Praise for *Wild Horses, Wild D*

The poems in *Wild Horses, Wilc* in a taut phrase, social movements in an incident, insights in an image. To follow the arc of Hough's life through these poems is deep pleasure and deeply instructive. "*... all we live for is perhaps pulling things/apart to see how they are made—& trying to approximate another's desires.*" This wise poet pulls apart experience—from giving birth to weeding perennials to insomnia—all filtered through the lens of fully engaged consciousness.

> LOUISE STEINMAN, author of *The Souvenir: A Daughter Discovers Her Father's War*

Language is a wild system, a wilderness. Lindy Hough follows her words along the path of the poem, trusting her ear, taking refuge in the language, probing wilderness. We follow, through intellectual, cultural, and personal histories. These wild horses, wild dreams—she's become wise in the making of her poems.

> BOBBY BYRD, author of *White Panties, Dead Friends*

Here's the arc of a whole life given to poetry, thought, and feeling, what Lindy Hough has lived and imagined her way through up to now. The work in these pages is powerful, vital, daring, liberating, and essential. Read this book!

> BILL ZAVATSKY, author of *Where X Marks the Spot*

Wild Horses, Wild Dreams begins with poems which search for identity and answers to life's fundamental questions. The volume ends with an acceptance of life itself, as in the captivating, "Thursday Night at Saul's." In her musical language, Hough creates in her reader a passion for the wild horses of life, or unpredictable reality. This, and the rest, is an insightful gift from a *griot* and major poet who has traveled far.

> CECIL BROWN, author of *I, Stagolee*

Lindy Hough has written a remarkable book, which courageously investigates the integrities that comprise a self. In the earlier sections Hough swirls within a disjunction of articulation and abstraction, addressing relationships with the past as well as her individuation and commitment to society, family, and spiritual practice. By the New Poems, she knows to fend for herself; poetic and spiritual influences are absorbed. The language is direct and lyrical—a distillate.

> DAVID GITIN, author of *The Journey Home*

Also by Lindy Hough

Poems
   Changing Woman
   Psyche
   The Sun In Cancer
   Outlands & Inlands

Anthologies
   *Nuclear Strategy and The Code of the Warrior: Faces of Mars
   and Shiva in the Crisis of Human Survival*

Wild Horses,
Wild Dreams

New and Selected Poems 1971–2010

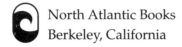

for John — with love &
admiration,

Lindy Hough

Lindy
ann arbor
7/24/14

North Atlantic Books
Berkeley, California

Published by
North Atlantic Books
P.O. Box 12327
Berkeley, California 94712

Cover photograph © Igor Terekhov/istockphoto.com
Cover design by Susan Quasha
Interior design by Paula Morrison
Printed in the United States of America

Wild Horses, Wild Dreams: New and Selected Poems 1971–2010 is sponsored by the Society for the Study of Native Arts and Sciences, a nonprofit educational corporation whose goals are to develop an educational and cross-cultural perspective linking various scientific, social, and artistic fields; to nurture a holistic view of arts, sciences, humanities, and healing; and to publish and distribute literature on the relationship of mind, body, and nature.

North Atlantic Books' publications are available through most bookstores. For further information, visit our website at www.northatlanticbooks.com or call 800-733-3000.

Library of Congress Cataloging-in-Publication Data
Hough, Lindy, 1944–
    Wild horses, wild dreams : new and selected poems, 1971–2010 / by Lindy Hough.
        p. cm.
    ISBN 978-1-55643-962-9 (alk. paper)
    I. Title.
    PS3558.O844W55 2011
    811'.54—dc22
                              2010038793

1 2 3 4 5 6 7 8 9 UNITED 16 15 14 13 12 11

For Richard

and my children
Robin Grossinger and Miranda July

CONTENTS

Preface

The poems selected from my first four books show a young writer coming into artistic surety and locating herself within a poetic lineage.

These poems map, among other things, the movement of place, one of the important parameters in the poetic tradition I was part of. It was defined by many poets, preeminently Charles Olson. Also important to me were Robert Duncan, Gerrit Lansing, Robert Creeley, Robert Kelly, and Denise Levertov. We published some of these poets in *Io,* the literary journal Richard Grossinger and I started with friends as undergraduates at Smith and Amherst in 1965. *Io* was the basis of the publishing company that became North Atlantic Books.

The Io Poetry Series commemorates this union, by publishing some of our colleagues. I'm pleased to be a part of a group which was so influential on my own work.

Although a common concept now, I first heard Robert Kelly talk about the phenomenology of space from Gaston Bachelard's *The Poetics of Space.* I was influenced by this notion of *locus* in these years—the mid sixties.

This school of poetics, which picked up strong currents from Pound, H.D., and William Carlos Williams, became known as New American Poetry, after the influential and helpful anthology *The New American Poetry,* edited by Donald M. Allen in 1960. I headed off to Smith College from Denver in 1962; this group of poets had became central to me by junior year.

Mt. Desert and Portland, Maine, are the locus of *Changing Woman.* North central Vermont is viewed in *Psyche* and *The Sun in Cancer,* and *Outlands and Inlands* slings between Vermont and Northern California.

The books develop an artistic vision out of the daily struggle to find a viable persona—among the entanglements of marriage with its joys and travails, new motherhood, the working out of confusions between artistic friends and lovers, life in a small town and the metropolis, and the difficulties of dislocation and relocation balanced by travel and exploring different places to live.

Inquiry into how the Mind works and differs from the soul or brain is a theme in the long narrative poem *Psyche,* represented here by three of its six Books. *Psyche* is a "working out" or "setting out," as the Victorians used to call it, of the myth Erich Neumann described in *Amor and Psyche: The Psychic Development of the Feminine.*

The character of Psyche manifests a sparky feminism partly influenced by being around Ed Dorn, who was writing and publishing *Gunslinger* at this time in oversize newspaper editions. I edited *Io/19: Mind, Memory and Psyche* in 1974, the year *Psyche* was written. Robert Duncan was rediscovering and writing about H.D.'s *Helen in Egypt* at this time, which I read at the suggestion of Robert Bertholf, my field faculty member for an M.A. at Goddard College. *Helen in Egypt* became the prime influence on the form of *Psyche.*

The new poems over the next decades sampled here kept flowing these concerns into new waters, creating new streambeds.

from
Changing Woman
(1971)

Moral History

The notion is foul.
The notion is not safe.

Fail-safe.
Foul safe.
fair play.
Safe play.
Safety.
Play safe.
Fail play.
Fail through play.
Play through failing.
Playing at riding a bomb.

Failure, a more adult
word. Connoting degree,
general condition, act not
so demarcated as Fail.
He fails, but is moving
towards (inexorably, like
a giant snowball) Failure.

Pass. Northwest Passage.
Loveland Pass. Berthoud
Pass. Northwest Failure.
Power Failure.
Powerful failure of fail-
safe devices to obviate death.

We Grow

SUSPICIOUS of every word,
as of every breeze. How mean,

I was thinking, of my thought
about him, & instead of mean

meant small, cruel, a strong
emotion after throwing a negative at him.

Because I had thought: the disease
is bigger than him. Finally takes him

over; something at last is larger
than him: his body, the disease in it.

He had only the flu. But mine was a mean
(cruel imprecise sarcastic irritable jealous)
thought, as if to say with delight—
finally, you're down. Your brilliant mind
can't work against the physicality of the flu.

He answered this:
                    There are truths.
                    I'm one of a lot of people, small
& yet moving, coming to these truths through my own
means—narrative, stories, poetics, a poetic.

Others come to them through other means.

He held up the yoga book he was reading, a man lunged on the
cover stretched out over his feet. Biology. Yoga. Astrology. I read

4

about others' means, & try to take in some of them, but it is never a case of the largeness of me & whether I win or lose. There are *universes*—I just keep going.

He had himself correctly lined up. A star in the nightlight sky full of myriads of stars in galaxies in universes. Not the only largest or particularly large; correctly spaced out about size.

A Phenomenon

            :   when i cared about you
i was concerned: whether you got off
Librium, what you wd do when George got back,
how you will learn to stop crying.

But it's floated away now: stars have wheeled
& new boats have moved in &
that distracting track across the fields
has rammed into me again; it was a pipe dream
to think of getting there fast as an
airplane, crossing land through a cloud
of illusion.

            That's why every day has
a different garden in it: not only
different vegetables to plant, but all
around my land the terrain keeps changing
as I look at it closely, the spots change
soon as I have worked over them, let drop
some incredible energy and involvement as
I plant them, different ships to be dealt with.
But they all dump into one pipeline,
& baby, *that's* what sustains,

                        not my altruism
for you & your crib, velvetpants, eyeglasses
spiderdance.

Irresponsibility & Its Blanket, Non-Attachment

                Some days I work in the garden all day
& some days I say fuck it.

& I'm still happy,
God's in his heaven, if
the grass is greener
on the other side I'll never see it
or will be of another consciousness
if I do.

                God the *horloger*.
                Our careful keeping of God's time
                by our chronometers.

Does he care enough
do we of his
to keep our time
to reckon it

Does God even know
or care
that we are human.

We are petulant
in our humanity. The baby
cries across the street,
unsure of All & Everything
except that Sun's uncomfortable on
his head or belly, burp/gas/air
the air you breathe you can exhale, people,
makes me cry.

Two ways (like looking at God's watch)
to kindle a look at the apple tree.
He's an old man in distress. Gnarled &
sick, dropping premature apples which
could be rosy round red America. Help it.

Or, that's the way it would go, untouched.
Let it be taken over by the bands of wilds.
By the Wild family, nourished on goat teats
angelic hands & ears & eyes
will help it cross the Androscoggin.

Apples, I love you green & small
or wormy
or not at all
or red.

Two Bands for Robby in June

Did you learn all this before you came here?

That really is the question, isn't it?
How long are we going to be alive,
& what shall we do until we die?

I put you to sleep & still I sleep deep,
while you pull apart a book that asks
for it, is clearly mechanical object
rather than flat, something must be
done to that contrivance, you think,
and destroy the book in the process.

But new is nothing. It still says
CAR & still says TRUCK, and all signs
point to it still being a birthday present
for you, just what you are talking about.
& so we give it in a slightly irrelevant
form, because we move quickly and don't
take much time at what we do.

> all we live for is perhaps pulling things
> apart to see how they are made—
> & trying to approximate another's desires.

*   *

I thought I would draw you a truck
& a train
& a car thrown in
because truck and train are hard to say apart.
& show you them, but you grabbed the pencil

away and didn't want to be shown anything,
wanted to make your own drawing,
or not.

How the stars do fall.
How the night air shifts the rain.
Pulling up cod, hand over hand,
Wendell in easy natural rhythm,
balanced heavily between his two feet having
done this since he was 11 or 12, thirty or
forty years of it, it's that way, you can't break
natural rhythm. To only sense the natural
rhythm, know the pulled stop that means
fish biting & not caught on a boulder, to go with that
tug always, confidently

I watched Wendell's form & tried to mimic
it, right hand doing just this, left hand this high
began to feel sometimes I'd caught something,
but had to let him take the line for the real
proving tug, pronounce it fish, he'd maybe say,
"I think you've got something there" & give it
back to me for the tugging, the excited pulling
of it heavily up, hoping the line would be loaded,
taut physical strain of
reeling in. White arcs through the ethereal water
at the side of the boat, first one fish, huge,
then another / another.
Hook off, & plop
into the boat.

The Dinner

        an older couple comes to dinner, they
are beautiful at the door, a child behind a big cake,
wine strides in & presents itself, but they
tarnish.
        They argue incessantly—
when forced
to confront each other directly
it's a smashed wall, finally
a coda: a mounting pitched laughter
mocking the other whether he
or she
lies with strangers;   she allies
the child against his dad & they whistle
together while he tells a lobster story,
the sarcasm piles higher & higher
until my ears are stuffed with
stale barbs, the malice in their eyes
crowding like a third eye

        doing dishes:

        you were nervous while we
        argued, weren't you?

        damn straight

& demeaning—she to her husband who has enthusiastically
laid his story in a long roll across the floor:

        pick up your scribblings, Lynnie,
        its time to
        go

Storm off Isles of Shoals

Solid & stolid & sea
spent, the brunt of
the storm never knows
where it will
let up, had enough,
at whose door did
it linger & pass on,
mad wolf into the
night, gone hunting
over onto someone
else's shoals,
someone else's
ocean dream   tide
                         & continent

So we argue; & next morning
find bright sun tossing snow
storm
blown out to sea

Indoors

I am so up-tight,
strung-out,
his scattering of
the jar lids all across
the kitchen floor while
I dodge them to make dinner

lurches me into
a vestibule of
knotty tears;

        push, like
the hot air making
its way up the stairs
from the pot
bellied stove,

        myself, up to
cooler regions, where he
sleeps in calm & I
restock, make a circle in
the cold window glass
frosted
so we can't see out.

Frenzy of snow
I can only glimpse
out of a corner patch

blowing up & out
& all about, we
moor ourselves

more closely to book,
needle, typewriter, as
snow density dares us
to drop anchor in
the cathedral of
Inside Us

Ocean Perch

(out of water

eyes burn
scales ache
shadow-territory melted
to pain, to end
of all known world   to blinding
flash of a
glint of silver
here I ascend
to the long-ago remembered:
Once I was fish
& it was
Water
all I knew needed & loved

(in water

All
is potential. I
glide & swerve
know best every
negative capability.
Only my shape, everything the sides
of my head see
is form.
Kelping sinuosities
define my thinking.
No one knows
more the
sweetness of movement
the horror of totally
still.

We Go to Rome Again

A week of distrustful servants
slipping & sliding all over the
mind's eye. They were slipshod,
hardly held together, their shoes
constantly coming off, having to
run to me to pound them
back on again, such an ordinary
smith.

These servants were informing
on the days of the week. Trying to
get them to accept bribes; graftology,
the simple science of screwing
someone not your own. The days,
thus informed, were all the more
in the know, holding, as they
did, the actual key to our progress.
We could not go forward without
moving through Tuesday, &
after that Wednesday, onward
to the Arno. That is,
if we ever reached it.

The masters of our fate
held our bridles in their slippery
fingers; we were afraid the
whole month would head down the drain.

We were collective.
Or saw ourselves so.
Spawned off from the eldest of us,

we were always children, or became so
on this continent.

           The guide
(his name hard to pronounce &
easily forgotten) called our attention
to the movement of earwigs
balanced on the corn stalks.
He would have us notice the
rustle the mold made,
snuggling up to the stoned limas,
drowned in passive soggy soil.
We accepted his explanation that water
was the cause of the limas' damping-off
(an otherwise form of death)
& we accepted his explanation that
earwigs were divorced from ears
because he was one of two screwable
men in town & we had been keeping
a sharp (an eagle eyeing a
mouse, or a mouse eyeing a dragonfly,
or a dragonfly eyeing a gnat)
I
on him.

          But he kept at a level of
formality that was intolerable,
& finally we blended into the
group, &
settled back to watch
the sights. At home perhaps
it would be different.

But it never is:
what's There is
here;

we are surprised to learn
that some European countries
have supersonic transports flying
faster than the speed of sound
& dope & exploitation of women and children
that ours is not the most deluded family
on the block.

We saw ourselves sick
of the sights &
sick of opportunism
& sick of rain
    in Rome.

The Flower's Space

Gloxina Blue Chip, it's hard
to invent a story that wd be right
for you. A situation in which
you wouldn't be the fail-safe

integer, the plot without which all
blank spaces fail. As though you
needed a situation, a garden plot
all your own, required a new day

each day, beaten down easily early
in the morning if all fails to
reveal itself new. Some buildings
have to be left standing: the patient

inventor can't approach a totally
different cosmology each morning.
The barn still stands: sled on
patch of brown ground surrounded

by snow, hockey stick against
garage. But the light is changing
all the time, moving across the
snow fields sun ages but little

in its eons of agelessness. Old
age ceased to care. So firm, in-
firmity is not a concern. Simply
unconcerned with unknown white space,

or dark star-dotted black. Columbus
thrown in jail by an
ungrateful king and queen,
Will West after the pages end, making his
way on the other side of the Mississippi.

You understand, don't you Gloxina:
I want to give you a tiny pot so you won't
know this loneliness that comes not
from not having *others* but from

having *The Other* constantly on one's
back (a wicked book, a wicked man),
constant unbroken looking of

the tiger in the face,
the whiteness of the uncharted
sea & sky. Never a let-up
in the azure rain.

Confusions of Place

I'll not admit when I lay sleepily the
cadres of cheerleaders turning cartwheels of
drowsiness in formation on my eyelids, thinking
of wide flagstone terraces in back & brick porches
in front with yellow stone bears & white benches
a winding shiny wide mahogany banister
arching inside a curved staircase, 19 stairs,
sliding down scratching it with a belt buckle;
a soft sunken turquoise pool with goldfish in it
some summers, the paint flecking off, the drain
stopped with a red plastic cup which caught its own
leaves under the junipers; a grape arbor with a
fountain that never worked but grapes and vines
on which the cat lay, suspended over a play-
house, dappled in sun patterns which fell
on the slate floor

that I'm thinking of my childhood house, shell of
early years, phenomenological shell of
later images of *house*. The quiet tyranny of those details
orders my mind's caravans on trips forward & back.
The house slices time and has lovers, of which
I want to be the best, the most faithful. Certainly
the most adoring. I people it with bruited occupants.

A lovely regal lady has possession of the house.
She glides in velvet, purrs with a velvet tongue
to its windows; her hem, sash, & slippers polish
the stairs as she flies down them. Up and over
the staircase endlessly she finally throws herself
out by night into the courtyard between the two towers,

becomes a bat: we see her on hot nights
tearing by at an erratic jerky clip of speed
birds don't do. She claps her hands.
The house blurs & wobbles, rings itself
with green smoke. Our four cats come out on the
high flat tar roof & peer over the edge, running
in worried little steps between the past
& the present.

          The house slipped from my parents'
hands as they slipped from each other, the years
pulling them apart as easily as an Oreo cookie,
until now they live separately one in an old basement
apartment and one in a new highrise.
Streaming down out of a century
of living, my mother comes to rest beside swimming pools
with community game rooms & rules on
pets & children & women, as my father floats
down the canal to the Platte.

          Can that regal bat lady
fulfill that house's power? How does one
make a house happy when its family is grown
and gone? Surely the Linden tree in
back sighs each fall, *Where is she who was named*
after me?   Surely the pool remembers and says
Where? She patched my cracks every spring. She
worked to get me sparkling.

          The house sighs for
all the power it had, & doesn't know of its
power over me. There are branches off this root:

No one can find out what happened to Minou Drouet,
blind French child poet my father was taken with, &
thus I was too, who occupied a pocket of my childhood,
except me. Only I
can track down her piano-playing Loire forests,
even remember the families of birds who nested
in her sleepy hair. Is she married to a professor
in Paris? Does she live a civilized happy life
of maids & children & appointments? Is she *very*
unhappy at losing the piano-playing forests?

Afternoon

a voice sings The National Anthem
& we are poised for the play-off.
Something is about to happen.

He flies from here to there, isn't it always
like that. Roots are where we return to,
what we try to hack up & fail at, are too tenacious
We give up & turn truth into magic.
& they do care, watching him watch the game,
I decide it is pure concern. There is no
trickery or fakery here. For a rough sport,
it's a clean game. There are very few questions
of human motivation to consider.

Later, friends come, eat, drink, have a party.
Afterwards I feel unspeakable let-down,
we clean up with sadness: there was no real
communion, un-invited guests came & hogged the
persimmons & pomegranates, talked to no one else
but each other. We want to feel free but only
feel indignant, we were rice grains shaken
in a colander, softly passing.
& No one touched anyone else, no one met
any one's thoughts. Those I had imagined myself
speaking quiet meaningful spirals to were across
the room spouting loud trivia, as I was also.

Emu Ritual Dance

We sing about their dance
from the sunshine of our day
as they sing about the emu.
He is a large feathered bird
big of bowl body, long sinuous neck,
tiny head with eyes-that-see-so-far.
Majestic, he is focus of
the dance.

The process is many-fold: the bird is
made sacred. The work of the dance
is sanctified anew. The badlands (the
Place Itself, or our place in the sun,
& what that might mean)—in this case
one tree, scrub, dry caked earth of
lizards—is made sacred.

A spot of ground is made wet to a rich
burnt sienna, then dried & smoothed.
As it dries the colors are mixed:
ash is scraped for black,
blood is spurted for red.
Where does the white come from?
It's in a trough; a board hollowed
(hallowed) out; the painter dips
his stick in & presses white dots
in patterns around the bent arrow tracks
of the bird. Dust motes? Snow?
Fine spirits?

The men know each other well.
Their connections to one another
are strengthened by this dance.
They rub the black ash-paint on one
another's body. Painted, some cheer
& jokingly criticize, some act the story out.
All know how it should be done. There
are past performances to compare with
this man's stance, the way he shakes
his body.

The hunters have gigantic head-
pieces. They feel that weight, not the
weight of all universe & responsibility,
but the seriousness of the catch & the dance.
It is not awesome, although their bodies
are full of trembling. Their motions are
exact & definite.

The movement underway, each feels
the oddity at seeing the others like this.
He is his everyday self, yet he is Another with this
huge mask. The hunters assume
their positions in the bush,
the emu-man at the waterhole lowers himself
carefully, each muscle straining.
        He takes a
long slow draught, then stands upright. A slow
shudder convulses his upper body, which shakes all
in one piece. He is big strong Beautiful Bird,
totally revealed & exalted.

It says in the titles: *this film is not to be shown within Australia.* We understand: for the white camera (another actor of another tribe) to perform the ritual on un-sacred ground would strike a profanity of severe fire.

Three Poems Greeting April & Maine

1

Easy as silk lying on new fallen frontier
April proclaims herself, rising, a rush
of heavy wings from
border-angels, pocket-pools; a chameleon sings
of faery seas

2

Flying back over finally only patched
snow-covered Maine we are quickly inland

try to see key roads & coast of Cape Elizabeth,
briny girl we would recognize & coax into

coming home but the terrain yields like a
dead body to anonymity. Wide road is wide road,

planned oval of certain Scarborough Downs madness
is terrain cut/fried/liced, farms & woods

interact their own social behavior
only look down, over see, plane's

shadow is the Doll's toy all below is meant to
be, a cool sunny day below the clouds.

3

Jealousy envy & excitement
from trying to do

another's work
is soon dead
& boring.

Rain drips
into dark cloudy day,

only seen
when I focus on air

at angles
involving distance!

Make it alive
(a furry animal
reaches inside its skin)

coming from inside the self,
a scaffolding and structure

there, on the shady side of the street
in the anguish of vanishing elms.

*

A boy in class says his pay from his very good job
in the West Detroit munitions factory helped him buy
a new car. In his next paper, he proposes war
as a shrewd & realistic way to eliminate excess people:
In his third paper he says if the guaranteed

annual income
were in effect, he'd
spend his time gardening & painting.

Who is this boy? I want to know him.
We have coffee and I listen to his veterans' tale
back from the war. He killed women and
children in rice paddies. Plenty of dead soldiers
notched on his belt.

Huge crashing boulder of appetite
cascading on angels' downy wings!

Mind-charging cascade of dope-peddling
angel breakers!

Did Hitler harden, garden, compost, find composure,
prune trees?

Too late for generalities
& too soon for specifics.
Going faster than I can handle.

The Vision of Serios

The World of Ted Serios: "Thoughtographic"
Studies of An Extraordinary Mind, by
Jule Eisenbud, M.D.

All the world's books sing a song,
a cacophony of sound a rustle of
bird wing of tree limb, this man
reaches up through
soil like new daffodil or crocus shoots
with stems reaching unconscionably far,
with a simplicity of movement & action
that belies perceptual mystic beautiful
raging torrents of
                          seeing!   This Chicago
elevator operator came out of nowhere, able to
throw pictures from his forehead onto
a screen. Came from where we're all trying
to get back to, came because
on the same beautiful spring day with opening of
buds & fields Kerouac bopped down a
San Francisco street with his black chick,
came because a specific dog shat on a
specific lily, came able to project pictures
out of his head of Queen Elizabeth, churches
in Rome, double decker buses in London,
crash bang into the outside of the within
of our scientific received notions of how things work.

Difficulty of getting the rocks out of
the vegetable garden, of getting psi phenomena
channeled into the brains of two billion empirical

scientists enough to take it seriously,
of pole-vaulting over The Great Wall
seldom traveled by Western man on feet or wings;
do we flow our bodies through spaces we can't tame?
Through time we don't know how to count?

All our rules break down.
Does the air carry pictures from waves?
Every nations' flags have gone silently down
at the same hour, never to come up again
until the world behind Serios' pictures
is totally revealed.

       Our language is too old,
our rules and experiments and phenomena too
deepened into great ruts, hackneyed & inflexible.
Still we call the farm workers
in China peasants, showing our lack
of familiarity with them,
but this is what *they* call them
in a feudal system.

       Chipping away
with experiments, with grass blades, it rains—
Serios & I get wet, the new Jerusalem was not
revealed either Tuesday or Wednesday. Such
patient laying on of hands, it takes. Such
ribald moons, totally new highsteppin' dancers.

       I grow irritated at the tendency of
the seedlings to damp off. No soil is pure,
no method is right unless
it is the most rigid careful one, seeing becomes
speech, expression transforms into communication
only after months of rules and elements of conformity.

These
many-varied soil-borne bacteria in their
amazing vascular web my eyes can't see
feast in complexity on anything, let out
all evil   to vitiate evil   as Crowley does occasionally,
only some very specific times eating human flesh—

The fungus feeds on the unfolding cabbage seed,
ringing it with a fuzzy base
before it's even turned from
green to white in the sun,
or straightened up. I give up. No medium
is completely sterile
          Are there wizards
& demons in Serios' head, a retina of untenable
ganglia growing on a mattress of
negative capability?

                    O mountains O seas
O stars of Maine over Central City mine dumps
where nothing was planted in the
mountainous tailings piles because nothing
was expected to grow;
embrace the incredible
ineffable mind of this small powerful man Serios
who is not bespeaking war or politics or peace
or famine or race relations or making any moral point
whatsoever about good or evil—embrace this mind with
a warm opening of arms, give him the City & the Laboratory
& several Gates for protection, let his heaven be revealed
                    & this man
be freed
knowing that others *have* heard & understood & told him:
Yes, you're doing it! There's no fraud here.

December: A Proposition of Movement

I am thinking of Christmas
whether to go out & buy gifts for my family
of how women shouldn't have to
        band together in flocks to get things done
I am thinking about 48 bombing sorties per day
        over the Ho Chi Minh Trail to stop trucks
        from loading & unloading supplies for a war
& of the land our house sits on—how at 4:30 p.m.
        the afternoon sunlight slants on the ball he
        has flung to me on December second, when it's
        not yet snowed   I tried to get Spindle
        grey cipher of a cat back into the house, chasing him
        only deeper into the woods; noticing the back of the barn
        which looks good where we started shingling
        blond wood over grey last summer
                & the duck house & chicken house which
                maybe we can have some chickens & ducks
                in next spring
& how maybe we can live here after all
although there is a ghastly war going on
& a new house building in what was a
soft glen with a stone wall before it
across Mitchell Road in Cape Elizabeth, ME
Even though the country is overblown a giant balloon fish
full of hooks too insensitive to even know the body of Christ

                Let the Maker be heard.
                Let the Soul's parts come together
                & violent acts cease for Limbo
                        & Rebirth

Let all who murder deer & humans & birds
circle endlessly if they do not renounce
           their unintentional intentional acts
make way for those who care for the
           land & Word & the Spirit tucked
in the souls of every living thing.

                    *   *   *

There is a man named Harry Coombs
of Peabody Coal Co. doing strip mining
on the Navaho Reservation at this very
moment. Let him mine his own body endlessly without
stop all his lives his spinal cord a corkscrew
anus filled with sand in burrows in caves in tunnels
an inept snake digging without surcease
Growing up in Colorado I have listened to the dirge
of this man all my shadowed life

Let the Holy Earth People grow powerful
& expunge him & his puny mechanistic band from
Navajoland   Make them fly   Let the Diné
again graze their sheep near open clean waters,
taking flight to the mesas when fall comes

There is a morphology of landscape
strong as the lines in a palm,
formed when the alphabet was shaped
by black birds flying ovals overhead
This won't be improved by any form of
strip mining

                    *   *

Let Behemoth reign.
Let the Seamonster come to us,
Let him spread his briny weight
            onto all our parts & days
Let the Lord of Light be shining
            Again
the stars embedded in
Our Holy Earth People's foreheads.

Portrait of the Father

> *To their young children, fathers are not wont to*
> *unfold themselves entirely, Pierre. There are a thousand*
> *and one odd little youthful peccadilloes that we think we*
> *may as well not divulge to them.*
> —Herman Melville, *Pierre*

Once I stood in a green bough
of family love, decorating the Christmas Tree
a few months before I
was to be married

& heard the incredible notion
that my father had been married once before
he married my mother
to a childish woman, he said,
wild & impetuous, it couldn't last
but a few months

in those seconds of realization
of another whole relationship
for my father, which spilled new worlds
of sunshine meetings & fall leaf picnics
into someone else's lap, he who was mature & routine
was not always so. "Her name was Mel," he said.
"Mel Flowers."
Mel Flowers? A name like that? I wanted to see her,
know everything about her.
Mysterious liaisons
& coverlets & tumbled sheets crowded my mind
watching him carefully place
our painted can lids & glued paper chains on
the Christmas tree, how like my gaze

at him to Pierre's musing stare at the
portrait of his rakish father
which he hung secretively, to get
it out of open light, in his closet

The jaunty air, caught in the portrait
as if he had just dropped in from visiting
the beautiful French girl; his buff vest,
the impetuous set of the dancing-figured neckcloth,
        "Love's secrets, being mysteries,
ever pertain to the transcendent
& the infinite"

"What was she like?" I asked.
"Oh, she was fun, but—kind of a goof. Your mother
was more—tough-minded."

"And that's what you wanted? More serious?"
"Yes. That's what I wanted."

        O star, O Christmas Tree of
fifteen childhood Christmases, O Father as Lover
(her and mine) in your own special world
of romance & mystery,
O infinite world of mysteries unfolding at the
hand of Fate whether we seek or not,
O world of the rainbow unknown &
moon world of the never but always possible
to know, prove to me that this life
I've been leading
has antecedents of more beautiful
mysterious nature, bells on hills ringing
I've heard only internally, in the back of
my invasive mind on quietest hilly nights in
moon-black verdure of summer . . .

A Botany of Love Poems

for Chris Lovell, who made me a pie plate
with the first five lines of this poem around the edge

1

We have made
our own pie.

We have baked our
own hands
into the pie.

They writhe, used
to dry air,
unused to clammy
cherry moistness
surrounding them.

There is no
choice.
We have
baked our hands into the pie.

2

I wanted
to take your arm
from the windowsill
of the car
as it left

carry it back
to the house
with me.
Perhaps I could
deal effectively
with that small
a part of
you. It is
about all I
could handle:
could apply all
the doctrines &
systems to
come out with
something that
makes us relate
more finely.

Alone
all there was left
was your song, coming to
me from a thousand
books over the years
I reached for that—
The part
you'd have me
have.

3

How each song
is only
one's own

how loving another's
body fights
the slippage into
another's system sheathes my body
like a hood
over the falcon's head.

you wd have
that I be turned on
to myself, rather than
Dante, Whitehead, yourself,
he whosoever has made a complex
for himself.

because models become
molds to fit into, crumble,
the competitive racer
loses to herself

How much you turn
to find the sun is all

4

At your reading
I could only get involved really in
the longer poems.

Time created there
to be enticed, unzipped,
played with, exchanges of
understanding to pass
back & forth, time for

the mind to rebel
& get a drink of
water & return

find still there
the same territory
no one gone home

       made happy that fix of
       multiple sectors: sex &
       science and Whiteheadian
       actualities converging
       in

a love act

The paper wasps
are trusting enough of
our eaves to
build their hexagonal combs
under them,
     Cover, they say, give us
shelter
be wind
breaker for us

Their engagement assumes
faith the house will stand

       day after day, they have that trust!
       That it won't be
       destroyed by fire or
       an act of God
       or Love

5

Love cares about itself
as process.
Love is not object.
Love is verb, the
acting & feeling of
tiny details which
hang together to make
a joyous
structure.

       Love demands
       an object.

The feeling is ancient. I
am treading such
a gnarled, rugged
path in pursuing
your forms, not knowing even
the time spans you use.
       Love is
pure abstraction except in
the prism of the body:
the desire mine feels for
yours, for the
vibrations you make in air
falling into my body.
       I care about the
broadness of your back
under my hand, not simply
your back, alone in space.
       Ursine energy. A botany
       of related synapses, teaching

the systemic inversion of
recycling tailspins converted
into fantasy, using
(carefully as glass, metal) longing.

6

Too close up
anything looks scary.
The fire across the road
tongued out of
the basement window
occupants gone hunting
the fire started after they'd gone.
Real torture
is to continue without end what
you've done most wrongly in life,
thus they will continually
rebuild their house through
life & Purgatory & Hell, fire chasing them
as they hide in the forest
waiting for the doe with her fawns.

Seeing more than autumn orange &
with ordinary reactions of alarm
we called the fire department.
Volunteers sped down
local roads to the fire house
just beneath our house
scattered, a hodge-podge of
hoses, couldn't find the hydrant,
finally got straight shots
trained on that fire.

Day in, day out   Each night that fire
stirred the brinkmanship energy
it aroused

        You arrived
        while the ashes were cooling
        interior of the neighbor's house
        spread all over the lawn, we ate
        coffee lobsters clams wine
        embedded beside the fire—
        now the intensity of you and it are so
        interchangeably mixed I find myself
        hoping for action & destruction &
        repelled by the intensity of your
        flame,
        I keep calling up your name in
        disaster warnings to Cumberland County.

7

        The whole point of the sexual fantasy
& the magical act, and close attention to
both rituals, is to sharpen the vision get
a detailed take or sighting from a loss of
perspective through immense magnification.

        thus the stronger the lens
        (close-up, mescaline, sacrifice
          of a cat)
            the stronger the Force, &
        (perhaps) the Vision

8

I circle
lie,
weep,
am frozen—
Sing.

i want you,
in tremulous divisive
differentiated
ways.   In
melting dripping lunges
which show
               what want is,
               what snow is,
               who you are
               & I am, &
               am not.
                        How I am you.
                        How your energy is
                        (or always, once
                        begun)
                        mine. "Cus I'm midway down
the midway
goin' down"

No one is alone
having once been
in the same room
with another.
               & yet with you
in the kitchen I
was silent, didn't
even draw on the

energetic selves which
hold me up, support me
Monday through Saturday.

9

Perhaps the most
delicious
            (& oldest
confusion
walks the silent
forest floor
is whether
        I want you, or
        the resources
                gold, metal energy (urgy
        I draw from you.

10

You come plainly.
                You come away
plainly.

            Light
                behind the rain
            makes the sky
                light grey.

    It is a plain grey.

    It tells the story
    of unfinished endings
    & suspended relationships.

The Filaments

We're both wound tight, separate threads
thrown out in the centrifuge
show dusky monuments of a binary code.

Messages fly in, above, and about relation:
mind-touching, I feel myself unwinding unevenly
thread running too fast from above,
lumbering around my parts from below

but it feeds into an interlocking pattern
where you too are ceaselessly unwinding,
no more able to stop your movement than
the sunflowers can stop their total buffetings
by the wind, a hurricane up from North Carolina
(arbitrary, as arbitrary as all weather & birth
& soul-life are) to which they must dance & flutter
ceaselessly, ruffled up with each new gust,
swaying, already tired because of such a heavy
        yellow head, bowed—

We pass each other, screaming particles of
honesty under our breath, dust motes on the thread
unseen by others but recognized by us as everything,

it is all in traveling: the particles of fog
before my eyes, the nodes of thought we bring
to each other & spill out in the work;
the progress, the movement which makes whole
items cohere, & a webby veil we can live in

Wrapped (rapt, like Odysseus & Diomede)
in schemes finally with one another &
the night's chicanery, we're encased in the same
flame. The fire is as horizontal as
time & thread only allow, traversing itself,

burning itself from one end to another & back again.
We're left whole, to any visible eye; stitches of
a great web, flaxen threads of Another Being's sails.

from

Psyche

(1974)

Book I

[1]

Everything is in it. Dancing, a man, a new place, a family, and all the old legends of family and family unity; all combine for her in an unraveling set of possibilities and stoppages. There is only one rule: that one be outside oneself.

Dancing; a form;
the form knows the way
into heartbreak;

can't skip to the shore,
find shell and clam;
Dancing, the form is limited

to movement before a mirror,
to movement before an empty
or a full house,

faces peering up,
a wash of blinding white light,
the dance unto the invisible eyes.

Chilling, when Mickey One
in that last final set
is able to sit down

and *play* that piano, the whole
city of Chicago opening out
as shivers run up and down my spine;

that's it. That's it. The beginning of
the beginning unto death, & isn't
that all that matters, Greek time

American time, these words I say
unto you: we all wanted to be born
and we were afraid to hasten our birth.

[2]

The studio has a warm smell to it; heated sweat as though the beads
fell on the radiator and were released immediately into the air, cooking
smells of twenty pairs of straining legs. There must have been a
romance to it, but was it inside her, or did it exist for anyone else? They
all came, like she did, so others must have believed.

Offerings to who?
Early learning that one's body
was the most sacred

& only instrument,
the mind totally subservient
to the leg, the height, the line

of the back, the arms.
No one spoke of the line of the mind.
The mind was to know

how to control the rest,
how to count music,
how to sustain the body

when it was finished
& folding up. Everything
always hurt, a ritual not complete

until pain was totally dominating,
and not begun until pain had begun.
The *barre*, the piano, the floor,

the mirrors, in every studio. They
are the same, some small variations
(in tone, quality, professionalism)

& yet the mystique is the mirrors
and the teachers. They are there
to fall in love with; falling in love

with one's self, one's lines, one's
image of perfection. *If I do very well,
she will love me,* breathe twenty

straining rib-cages. And she is reliving,
in each one, the tautness
the rest of her life has never held.

Psyche, who do you kid? You can walk through mirrors. She really did
love you, really did want to take you home. Why were you so curious
about where she lived, who her family from India were, the coincidence
of contiguity, that she lived so close to you in Denver and Central City?

My ballet teacher lived in a huge house
on Columbine and 13th Avenue,
a block from my grandparents.
They are all dead,

others live there now. No more Indian cousins,
no infatuated beginning student moving swiftly—
Her tiny foot, arched so high to show us

a white curved baby mourning dove
then crammed into black taffeta spike heels
no larger than the tiniest loaf of bread

I can bake. An orchid on her head
at the travelling troupes—Ballet Theater,
Ballets Russe de Monte Carlo. She needed

a playmate for the child from India my age.
I came to her house to play with her,
later to practice my court jester's dance

a part I did not like. I wanted to be
a sylph, a lady-in-waiting, but at least I had
my own dance.

I walked by her house
after school. Face backward: Denver.
Face forward: Plainfield cows grazing on hillsides.

Human geography—
beautiful particulars revealed
in the palm of a hand.

[4]

What was her house like? A cave, a tower? A bower? The base of a radio transformer, to which you ran once, escaping from school?

An old, blue, cool, stately house,
all I wanted, a house for purple
satin to come through

a house without mortgages but
perfect flowers
which she had not raised from seed

in egg-cartons on the window-sill to be
knocked off, and put back up
carefully again

a house where one walked quietly
because nothing was real.
It was beyond the mirror,

where you could go if your line
was good enough, to practice
your dance in the basement.

The embarrassment of not knowing
it, of having to wear a court-jester's costume
when I had the beginning of breasts

and wanted to be a maiden, long netted hair
in Greek pastel wafts like the older girls—
a court-jester with no note of mystery

but only jocularity.
I kept forgetting my steps.
I wanted to die

except she had taught me the mystique of
inhabiting a part—a way to live. The steps
kept leaving my mind; I wasn't breathing.

You can't live without breathing.
In that basement, I was afraid
of her tiny black spike high heels.

You couldn't speak in that dance.
Couldn't cry out.
Had to constantly check one's line.

[5]

When you watch yourself grow up in front of a mirror, can you enter
it? Pierce it, like your ears were pierced in college, shoot on rubber
gloves and slice it, cleanly as the lover slices water with a knife?
Extrapolating outside to uncover inside.

Building a fence
around the insides.
Inside are the cows,

the sheep, the horses. They
live there already, it is
the Christ child

has come anew. Angels and shepherds
watched him being born, everyone cared
with his parents, who made it happen,

helped and felt,
overcome with awe.
Why are we on one side

of the mirror, and also the other
side? What amazing gift do we have?
Can we usher

through ourselves what has been
delivered unto us to give
to the world?

The mirror demands these questions.
Some who watch it get nowhere,
slip forever on glaze ice, build

and people their bedrooms
with fantasies.
Those who pierce it

do with *travaille,* heavy work,
live within
heavy redemption.

A hard regime. Harder than the
abstinence form demands, or a perfect line,
because all internal workings are

within the mirror's grasp also.
The dancer is more revealed
style and intent interweave,

arch across history. Aware of tradition:
the Doctrine of Will, the Burden of Set,
the Burial of Achilles.

6

How strange. All the people who were sacred had also an identity in Greek society. They existed in the myth of your mind and your mother knew them from the newspaper. She had photographs from the society page of Miss Cushing; the film-maker was in summer stock. Your mother remembered his name as a young actor.

The Golden Door. Brakhage played
in a summer stock group in Central City,
and remained there for my mother,

locked in the pure white form
that was her smart memory.
In dream Miss Cushing lifts

my leg higher, she is pleased,
in the scrapbook she is on her porch
at Central City with her orchid on her head,

waving, next to her older frail husband,
Fred McFarland. "I am sorry for the artists
who, to recover from disorder, make the

journey to Athens," says Cocteau. An image
in your mind can inhibit you from seeing
your own visions, idiosyncratic, eccentric,

brilliant. And so the courses are made up,
the friendships begun & fantasized about,
we could do these things together.

Helen walking the ramparts
All Greece hates
the still eyes in the white face

The Trojan War was not only Achilles' story.
Helen was there too. H.D. wrote *Helen in Egypt,*
her view of the war.

7

Christmas. An entity, a day, a man, cards up on the wall, baked things,
stockings hung from the mantle, the snow strung out into the mind,
expectations which can never be fulfilled. How does one find meaning in
these days?

A season of inexplicable peace. But not for
everyone, in every country. Brown fields,
a brown cow, the stillness of a cold night;

that born was a man who would make
things right, for some. But hatred and jealousy
quickly grew up, the tale became two tales,

Hanukkah and Christmas. They both treasure
Light, sensibility, safety, but forgiveness
is hard to come by.

One's expectations on Christmas
are always too high, the smallest bit
of nostalgia & desire for human closeness

can become rote
Best to start it new every year, new traditions.
Get out of the house! Sled, shovel,

go visit someone. The neighbors have this
more down pat: open house,
people come to visit them

between 3 and 6 bearing presents,
walking carefully in a line,
whole families.

Robby, it has to do with
an incredible man who was born
& became great did a lot of good

But then others in his name
later created tremendous evil
you have to be careful, through the ages

[8]

It's interesting on Christmas day to
          take a trip
          into town
see where other people live
                what their scenes
are
                what they forgive
                to do without

The mom is a beautiful blond woman
figures in a tumultuous mythic drama
                lives high over
the Winooski

her children
sled with mine across the street

                We will go on
day after day here
no way around it
or her

[9]

She   All our parents in Southern California
        Look, these pink slippers

He   These pajamas
                    (he holds up a box of classic
                        pj's   a pair of high heeled shoes for her)

She   There will be phone calls this afternoon

He   The kids think this is Harry's Discount

                    out, out
                    up the hill the kids yell as they head
                    out with their sleds

        I leave,
        3 Tampax richer
        my Christmas morning visit
        steps over the laughing Winooski
                    this is my village
                    I've visited someone who
                        lives here too
                    who I like who likes me

[10]

"Old Zeus—

                    —Young Augustus"

1

                    You turn off Rt. 2
                        at the appliance store
                        go over the bridge &
                            through town, past the
                            two markets,
                        Bartlett's & Kellogg's
                        at the fire station
                        turn right
                            & then
                                    two telephone poles

on the hill
is our house
            we live there
        with high expectations,
                heavy dreams

not surrealists or social anarchists,

just trying to find our way
    some attempts at consciousness

what comes
        is from so far away
                ocean laps from another island

I have wasted time,
    twisted my energy
        been thrown by an impossible
                madness

to have placed essence
of the outer world
in the body and mien
of a local man!   But it's perhaps forgivable
what do we have, except forms and entities,
people come forward who one might have known
in a past life, one feels a pull —
        what is it? how can one know?

Once as a young girl with Mari Buerkle down the block
we got fixated on a boy visiting from Kansas
stared at him sitting on the steps in front
of his aunt and uncle's house,
watched him mow their lawn,
tricky, because it was a steep slope
Larry Larsen, better than any fantasy

We dallied around him, not so much flirting
as *soaking him up*
        listening to his Kansas drawl
        he was the only spectacular thing
        in our slow lives, that summer
                Born too late, for you to notice me,
            we sang, with The Ponytails

If we averted our attention
from these things
we would not be human—bad things happen
        think of the horrible town in "The White Ribbon,"
bequeathing a generation of strutting Nazis

Always I want my men
to be beautiful,
others to not necessarily think them so
I make them shine like water on granite
shimmer like web-caught maple leaves,
twisting in the breeze
they're best at their most simple,
when not over-complicating everything

> trying to hold together
> a daily dying world
> for themselves

2

> Sometimes I wake
> to the pear tree
> heavy with its lushness
>
> realize my mind is working well,
>> we go outside at night here to see
>> the stars   eyes groping in darkness
>
> the intensity of beauty
> is richly felt
it floods into my skin
oh my

3

There is a quest
that wavers between
specifics which mark out
a path,

and getting at those specifics
through imagery

One doesn't want—!

Oh leaf,
bend down & touch my head
with your impossible quietude

Book II

[1]

What is the pull of adultery? A marriage worn out? People get tired,
just run out of steam? Women's magazines, films, stories, dissect and
feast on this carrion. There is something about lonely roads, danger, the
cold of winter, needing to get warm, that heats the heart. The outside
relationship beckons mysteriously because of its complexity and knots.
Can you make beautiful interwoven plaits from synthetic rope? The
heart fools itself out of desire for power. The opposite of harboring the
seed (what Psyche is supposed to be concerned with) is jumping into
the fire.

Penny-candy, penny delights;
the skyline of Toronto seen from a picture-
postcard set of dollhouses on Ward's Island

So that all your actions are informed
with a desperation that breathes of
romantic existentialism, but is more

likely, before-the-seeing.
I think
to make knots

one must really
understand them.
I have slept in one bed

of extremity (she thinks,
gradually coming to consciousness)
& thus must sleep in the other;

"Either I am a sloppy lady
with screaming children cut off
from the whorls of life I see

all round me, or I am totally dominated
by … what is it …" the air chill
in this attic as she tells me,

clandestine even, the telling of it—
"… love … or that which makes me take
incredible risks …" & thus she

must be a sailor on a bounding sea, living an
external experiment (more interior,
less visible experiment unavailable)

to prove one is alive at all.
I am beset, she is saying, by a
mystique of persona

which will be my undoing, my unconscious is
walking down the street & I have to run
to catch up with it

It's interesting (she says with lassitude)
a raven asleep in red boots
dreaming of a lost sailor …

Her lover came up then & said to me
I have to shore up some walls,
and he meant you!

Meaning not, what's going on here? (He
knows she will tell me)—or interest in
the frame of mind of his beloved, but

I need to make sure you're properly
enslaved, even while I dally.
This is the opposite of

what is passing for liberation,
instead of being enslaved
in your own world, responsible

for making it alive
which over the years you've
chosen shaped made grasped built

you're now dependent on his
belly and silliness & whims.
A pearl in a jelly-jar

watching yourself
in love's grip
a movie-image of yourself.

The trees sigh,
the elders sigh with remembrance of
Susanna and her naked brightness,

while you noose yourself with still
another man's concerns. What rainbow
ever hungered to duplicate itself in

another briny sky, its mind so on rain
the conditions of the blowy clouds
the light & stillness after the shower ...

conditions relevant to its shining
& lasting. So   wow
thought Psyche and

sang this song to whatever birds
hopped down in the alleyway behind
the huge disused skyscraper:

At this sitting, forget
mindless passion. Forget
watching yourself be beautiful

or distraught in FBS Fashions.
Rather the gradual lighting of
successive flames of your own

power and deliberation moving out
into the world when it gets too small—
your man needing your prayers.

Darkness is your friend, brings
warmth of the round words falling
around your body / keep your eyes

fixed on the flickerings, in your tears
accept the separate
functions of men and women—

passive and active
at different times. You're
most at home when you

are proud of what you do in the outside world
& recognize situations and people who
are too small for you.

Bright cameo moon.

The uses of power, as snow falls on the electric lines, of dream as you meet the dreamed in the kitchen, of the mind's spiritual quest as you stare at the lover, wondering that he is incarnated into a man. These obsess Psyche. In dream she invokes a muse of her own choosing and does with it what she wants. It's a step.

What she already knows
is a rich tangle
of possibility.

Threading through
the lover's hair,
knot by knot,

living with him to unravel
the sequel to the mermaids.
Not always searching.

The quest beckons—
tunneling to comprehend,
churning through, and turning over the soil.

When Psyche was small
mineshafts
surrounded the house. They were *really deep*

if you fell in you fell like a lead weight
all the way down,
thousands and thousands of feet

to a quick death, which no one
dared discuss. Then her oldest sister
walked backwards, chattering to

her middle sister, and did fall
into the deepest shaft. Luckily, she fell
on a ledge, was hauled out

by the fireman's rope. It was the worst
occurrence that had ever happened,
in the life of this family.
People thought the ledge was a miracle.

Never walk backwards became a mantra
of her childhood, as in some families
never dive into a lake spoke of hidden

drownings and hitting rocks. They learned to
skirt the shafts and the piles of gold tailings
dotting hardscrabble mountains.

Still, it lingers, the notion of falling *very far*—
Alice tumbling down the rabbit-hole
into a different world.

The trick with consciousness is
to be *leading yourself*,
not walking backwards,

not kidding yourself.
Dealing is difficult
in a dishonest world.

The simplest, most dense people
are the hardest to handle,
they want the rhythm of pure force.

Sexuality is a force, as prevention of
catatonia; it can mine rich sewers of valuable
matter unused, unvalued, untransformed—

Reach a larger world
not through controlling
others

Will my child have a world that
makes sense to him? Food,
a place to sleep that's comfortable

when he's thirty? Can this man
my muse—become a friend?
Or is it always going to be ice cubes

while we pull up linoleum?

[3]

*Psyche had a god-father, a famous poet, but as she came of age as a
poet he became depressed by his own children. He sent silver spoons for
twenty years, but when she grew old enough to really need him, it
became clear that he'd never talk to her. Perhaps he loved her mother.*

Some men keep bees.
Some carry maps
but don't go anywhere.

Those who carry maps
& show others how they work
are valuable: the trees listen,

the doors bend and incline to
catch the gist,
the handles strain to jump off

and follow the map-tracing
with the red magic marker.
The trees don't care about rainbows

anymore,
or crucibles,
or witch hangings,

but maps they entirely dig
where there's a man with a map
he's going somewhere

maybe he'll plant more trees,
which in their gradual
growth of perception dig

that growth of form will further
their species. Let the map be honored
and let him talk about it.

[4]

Psyche: *Dreams command our attention because they offer an image from somewhere else with an accompanying emotion. Sometimes all you have is a still:* I was lying on the floor with a group of women dancers and we clasped hands. *To have the powerful image & connect it to consciousness is a kind of ethnography, creating an account which does justice to another way of seeing. Diaghilev to Cocteau: "Étonnez-moi!"*

The dream proceeds
with its ineffable reasonableness
like the 6 o'clock news

tanks glide in & out
bombers strafe
I strain to translate

a message to you
but am mainly fixed on
whether you will love me,

this dream is solipsistic.
Sense in the western world
flies off the handle,

the words ring themselves around.
Amour & Achilles
await our revelations

At the college the faculty fight
for power like the Greeks at Troy,
crazily, not caring about the College as a whole

A father thousands of miles away
in the reasonableness
of his Protestant ethic gives

his daughter in marriage to a husband
the daughter still wants the father
& what an unrequited love scene that is—

He pulls back so much the daughter
loses him almost altogether,
distance makes strangers of them all

& then he dies,
too early, unexpectedly.
She is stricken, bereft, and begins—

haltingly, because she's not good at it—
to search for him in the Seven Planes
of Consciousness.

The West Virginia hills with their strafed strip-mined landscape,
secondary forests all, reach higher, trying to act like reasonable
adventurers. The cows look up to check out the landscape, make sure it's
still there. They are worried they'll be stripped too of food. The natural
world is collapsing fast.

    & I really like milk.
without hills no trees no grass
no cows no milk.

We can eat plants.
We are chasing each other
round and round

in a mad dirge,
a roller-rink
leading nowhere.

I have fantasies of encumbering
myself with babies,
you have dreams of nursing at

so many women, they are streaming
after you. Still,
around. There was a particular

century in the Middle Ages
where earthiness was proved to be
a cover for a totally anti-spiritual

attitude, & I don't mean those
pious fish-headed Church Fathers who
burned witches.

Simply that the light
that fires the spring in your step
could be seen only as sexual,

or why Molly Bloom lights very few
candles in my temple.
The woman as supplicant,

on the other hand, as in Puzo's *Godfather*
Yes! the inner ship, saying the prayers,
holding it together by a light touch

so the whole life of adventures
spins out like a long carpet
with only a finger-push,

and the woman knows her place
is Great.

[6]

Ladies, get a hold of yourselves! All is not a dollar sign, a glass of wine, Tangiers, or Bombay. Everything comes back to the Golden Ass. It's ok to be hungry, but it's demeaning to be starving.

If you look at me,
I'll vanish.
You'll see,

there, you did it,
now you'll be sorry.
Although it is not

terrific either
to be invisible.
The not-revealed

has its drawbacks,
chiefly inscrutability.
It's hard to talk

from an immersed position.
All comes up bubbles.
The waves are not very clear

coming in, either.
Distortion results:
            BRAIN WAVES

It's easier
just to go about
one's business.

There never was any meeting.
You're making it up.
Something happened in your head

that occurred nowhere else on earth,
a stoplight that absolutely
no one saw but you

It's not embarrassing,
just hard to explain.
Like—how to begin,

when there's no alphabet,
no precipitation in the sky
to arrange the clouds in skywriting.

No fire to make smoke.
Dangerous isolated mute position
makes mutes. Makes

mottled mutations among the natives.
Makes atavistic music
more resemble monotones than silence.

There's an airplane coming but again
no body can see it but me,
and it's mainly mealy metal.

Psyche lets it all whirl around: outside and inside her mind. She's not afraid of the total goal, but the parts—the outside world, Amor's demands, family, work—must not impinge on one another. Each have their uncomfortable scenes of sinners and purged, spiraling up. The economy must slow and she must learn repose and peace.

Amor comes up
knocks on my skull
what's up there?

oh   not funny   no sense of humor
because it's *tonight*
the stop we all get off at

The crisis has always been now
Somebody likely to steal
plutonium from my soul, encase it
in a breeder reactor

make a really big bang
on his way to doing something
important   like forcing an issue
or saving a nation

The outside (doom, Bowie's Five Years to Live
economic world-market collapse
shortages of bread   fertilizer (nitrogen)
oil & gas reserves
& patience

lie alongside our desire to
make a family
which lies alongside my
continual desire to
make you
part of my crustacean shell

[8]

*Psyche wonders, who's controlling Cupid? Who would be so stupid
as to have him in their employ? How would he help the most seasoned
mover? Is it the wind, always preening on the set? Her sister's husband,
who is her dog's father? Cupid looks confident but has nothing together.
He runs a lighthouse & needs a way home. He repairs watches to pass
the time.*

He speaks:

Yessir
I have you
I'm the one you're crazy for
white knight
knight errant
knight tonight
totally uptight knight
glassed in armor
leaded in metal
encased in a glass helicopter
dropping glassine envelopes
        layin' only girls on the move
the noise of his motor is too loud

I'm the Superfly
the King's Eye you'll never find
I'm the one   you can't forget

[9]

sympathy for suicides
varies

        with the barometric pressure

        and

        Americans
        leave me cold
        only creatures
        attract

        there is a causal relationship here
        which makes for isolation

        which one can handle
        —careful
        of glass underfoot

An interesting domino theory

> She reads a set of word-magic
> which presses itself against her
> sleeps in fervent valley &
> writes this which she knows
> has bits of his poem which she dug
> floating sticks in a stream

> Another across the Great Plains
> reads what she wrote
> integrates it unconsciously
> into an essay about something else entirely

> which he reads to another
> This man somewhat bored, not particularly
> enthusiastic
> is nevertheless marked, as earth is carried around
> & strewn by his shoes without his concern

> He becomes dimly aware of a notion
> nostalgic in its sweetness
> which is wet   he grasps at
> it, writing a song which he thinks
> is about what he was dreaming last night

> but the original crumb is there,
> stuck in an image which a print-maker
> three states away hears over the radio
> while rubbing the stone with water

Watching the oils run into shapes he remembers
a romantic sequence he often goes back to
in muse   he rubs with a particular motion
which a woman feels down deep
in her living room ten years later
she sees a ghost horse
flying across the sky
& since her very being merges with horses
so easily she watches them drift
in a wavy line into the sea

Later she writes about the horse next door
bucking out its hind legs
    as it circles its pen
bored & restless   rushing in a fast canter
up to the fence and then screeching to a
stop in a cloud of dust

       "Ghost horse"
she thinks, not knowing where that comes
from—a cloud of a horse flattened, legs dangling
against the sky?

She's excited: no "irritable reaching after fact
and reason" here, dwelling happily with Keats'
mysteries and doubts she feels
part of a Great Chain of Being,
original notions coming
through distances and generations

Intimations of a lovely beatitude

She understands she'll never know the
archaeology of her ghost horse
no matter how hard she digs directly

She strides, covering great hectares
inadvertently & indirectly
faithful to Mystery.

Book III

[1]

Psyche travels with her family: Montpelier to Montreal and Toronto>points west. The towers of the Midwest are a matte flat grey flannel. After living with Gurdjieff in France Margaret Anderson felt the vivacity of the 20s and 30s slide down in America to now, the America I and my generation know now as the sole hopeful reality. Is the present vacuous, only the past energetic? Can the future improve only if it takes a parabolic backflip backwards?

More than *petites madeleines*, or whatever
object triggers the past's vibrancy—
as humans age &

realize that the world produces
ever more information to be absorbed
at the same rate that it produces

self-destructive capabilities,
will a person's life and actions become
a continual recital of pleasure in the past

or can people keep making it new,
creating new works?
Those who were interested in creating
will make new work, those who want to
live in their past will do that.

The future has the possibility of always being better than the past. We're not doomed to repeat the grave mistakes of history.

Psyche: Where I stitched his torn jacket cross-tracks meet at the corner of a pocket. His hand enters at that tangent. My kind of love for him is based on the emotions that pivot on this small square of green. Only I wear the jacket now because he got a new one. The railroad of completion that is my love for him surrounds now my own hand!

The trains through Kent, Ohio
often, loud, and regular—
with serious intent.

The day hammers away.
We move through it easily
with some suffering

we expect it
& want to learn to suffer with will,
feel with all being,

as Gurdjieff said:
*Such suffering that it will help
make conscious; help to understand.*

There's just no sense at all in
repeating the same stupid errors
from lack of self-reflective knowledge.
Get it any way you can: critical theory,
therapy, spiritual work, but don't
bumble along imposing your trip
on everyone else.

Real life depends on other human beings
not just on self, Gurdjieff said.
So there are islands

in this day, of happiness &
despair among billows of space
wherein *not quite* is the prevailing feeling.

The mind lurches ahead
like a slinky arching down the stairs
coming to rest in a neat pile.

Rest a bit; plans & schema
will flood back.
We stagger uncertainly

within this circle
of our own making,
a Bolivian donkey ridden uphill
& down
by some fool crazy prospector.

[3]

How mysterious to be on a trip moving around the country staying with
friends, glints of attraction in friendship; thinking of a man who must
identify with a stream, his main preoccupation moving, and wonder—is
he connected as stream is, to a larger cycle of snow melting from rain,
clouds sucking up from lakes, moisture glistening in the air? Does he see
these larger cycles, or simply glorify his fast-paced movement? The
figure of a man running across the whole fucking continent.

Against the wheat fields,
the vast plains of Canada
the vast plains of the Midwest

dark running figure.
Superfly,
Butch Cassidy.

You're the pusher man.
Our main man
because you can't think

of what else to do;
mind's a blank. Try
to see your way out of this.

Don't you dig that it's an
interconnecting set of links
from cosmos to tiny earth worm

this can blast your loins apart
inflame your nasal passages with
red hot &

you could get that if you'd stay put
a minute, emit or get
some calm

as some women do by having children
though it fucks them in other ways
they get (to a greater and lesser degree)
some sure calm

that way. I have always wondered
what Pound would have said to a daughter
He did say to her

"Start something in Brittany."
Meaning: people a land,
dig that there are

worse things to do than devoting
one's self to further progeny

the continuity of the best of
knowledge & civilization
is more important than

the furs, the endless free fucks,
the cars
which come to nothing

A farm
a ranch
Hard work &

release

[4]

Psyche looks at herself: narcissistic. At others: engrossing. At the world: full of things to look at. She looks at her hand for a while and writes this on the heel of her palm.

To another:

You are

an obsequious desire
a razzled snowflake
a frazzled rainbow
blithe Caretaker
compliant Energy
a fern, polygraphed
edgy hyperboles
Antarctica's prayer beads
loving currents
a wayside flurry

delicious thought

5

I am on the trail
of the female muse
sd Psyche idly drawing
herself up to the Sun
like a drawstring bag
& he does elude,
being ever present
in my fantasies it is
only very recently
that I have dug the connection
the main line between
those microcephalic rocks
backstage
& my meandering
pursuit of this man

Who of course must resemble
where I came from

be rocks   mine dumps
have sheds & outhouses strapped
across his back
sport chicken tracks from his eyes
like marked fresh snow

know Protestant terror
at not being prepared
for the Great Beyond & thus
at this late date
be thinking existentially
although it's way past time

Have a copy of *THE GOOD LORD SPEAKS:*
        ART & BASEBALL
inside his furry jacket
be no more hip
than a horse tethered in too small
an area

It is interesting
to watch those who so connect to
the Word   but are
stupefied & dumb
in society   or

I get off on your writing
but hardly know what
to say to you in person

the artist as Maker & Social Being

the fantasized
& you as social reality

my hand shakes
heart beats too fast
blinding temple pounding blaze when
I lift up the phone to call you

Acting on the other side of the mirror
you in real life
are not you in my head

6

Can you believe / there will be a day / when this will not be the only subject, when stock markets and devaluation will open up a window, when the sun will peek in and that sun alone will be looked at? The phrase, "Endless poems, all about the same obsession" comes back like a weary track.

I am on good terms
with the intimate,   sd
Psyche, laughing
at the sun in her cup
not taking much seriously—
Revolted by the preciousness
of the feminine
but still engaged by those in-
timations the sun does on the fence:
that "we are so close"
without a word having been spawned

Amor stood
stretched   yawned   it isn't
like that for me he said.
The gunshots you hear
down at the corral
are running away over the hills.
Your nose is stopped up
leading the show
bending every mood's desperation.
All those voices
in your head
can you *name* them

be discrete for once?
Separate & label them,
wrap them triangularly
in waxed paper like the butcher
at the Safeway we're coming to?

Amor while saying this
expostulated also on
the outer fence enclosing
the position of geography, culture,
the microbiotic & assumed the whole
of society to be himself

The culture proceeding like a
giant peanut made up of moving parts
this path difficult
to walk through

[7]

One digs
fairly swims in!
the complications of   pure size

That one goes through these things

        romanticism & altruism
        squaring off & reeling in love w.
            each other

        taking it alternately slow & fast

        what an afternoon I spent   so mad &
        irritated all the time   I feel now,
        hours later all that bile resident still
        in my diseased & eaten body

        when will it drain out

Looking at yourself &
the icons you create out of discrepancies

        Sometimes strife is so hard he won't
        leave off talking to me unless I close
        my door (on a three year old) & feel
        then guilty but it leaves him a space
        to fall asleep curled up at the door
                Later I open it, kind of horrified
                        know, he'll wake
        in the middle of the night still
        hungry   a bowl of cereal/a piece of

bread all he'll eat, doc what are we
doing wrong
                    (are children worth it?
is life?
            What is titillating is still
            the unresolved

[8]

*Psyche watches the master stone print maker Will Petersen, his art
based on the principle that water and grease don't mix. The image is
drawn with a greasy medium which will resist water. All blank areas on
the stone are prevented from absorbing grease by applying a solution of
gum arabic and nitric acid. The stone is sponged wet, then inked with a
large hand roller in brilliant colors: clear sapphire, cobalt, cyanine,
azure. The moistened areas resist the ink, but the drawing accepts it.
It's sensuous, Mesolithic, the huge heavy stone inked repeatedly until
the build-up is enough to print. One fixes on the intaglio: the edges of
the figure begin to come out.*

Breaking through
the hold of Eros—
painful, but productive.

The moistened areas
resist the ink
but the drawing accepts it.

Making marks on stone.
Wind, air—the figure against
elemental forces.

Psyche walks to the back
of the stage, tired,
shoulders drooping,
legs throbbing, body totally

responsive to the mind's commands
ready to go again
I will always be able to smell

the sweat, see again
the wooden floor
where, again and again,

I went back to repeat
the sequence of steps,
stunned with exhaustion

but pushing the pointed leg
harder and higher, (somehow
in tautness & exactitude

to get it right

She will not try
the number again,
will let go, go home

do something else,
fine relief to be free
to forces other than

emotional & physical.
The play of history
reasserts itself:

12th Century China &
the dialectic,
the exquisite beauty of

interlocking conceptual forces
comes back like a heavy river
returning
to its dry bed

Thank god for a mind
which can find its way out of
darkness

I know a man
who is seeing his life in an
impossible
but common
dichotomy.

He wonders if we can become fruits of the earth
drop the bourgeois rationality
encases us
which we have used to stick our worlds together
run free & fuck gloriously

While he says this
he uses a rhetoric that is birds flying,
totally engaging
in its layered complexity
he cannot control or quench this
He tells of the British wartime poets
he grew up on: Siegfried Sassoon, Wilfred Owen,
and introduces me to Barbara Hepworth's
punching through the hole

Without this rhetorical style
which he would lose
were he to pull off his dream
of not having to deal with the knots
        & complexities
which make us only interesting
he would be
one more poor fucker crying in the streets
looking for America / lost to all spirituality

He's a slight bit older than me
from a more dedicated Marxist background
takes politics more seriously
than a huge billboard of the nation's
aberrations & constipations
or a mnemonic device, only as interesting
logistically as the runs batted in,
he sees himself
encased in a shell-white skull
(but beautiful shell!)
of fears and terrors we work daily to shore up
& seeks, as a good Marxist,
engagement in Work or at the opposite extreme
inarticulate sexuality

A woman in a Panavistic Italian movie
ragged and bosomy
salt of the earth
always there   feet planted on the ground
A rock
but always sexually available
in an underworld scenario
for him to drop down onto—

What a traveling salesman.
What a voyeur
of the feminine psyche
this man turned out to be

Bedrock civility
covering an outrageously obscene statue
refined through polishing
so it can penetrate

and titillate even
the most cultured (armored) viewer

The stylistics of his persona and sculpture
he wishes to undo & lose
They are cloying, like ideology,
as the narcissism of surrealism is,
yet without these he feels too bare
too revealed

To me they make an intellectual
artistic world
Lonely in housewifery, a village
where no one talks to anyone else
I'm a hungry bird
picking up crumbs in the snow

Outside in sunlight
and snow,
the children play

[10]

Oldenberg: "You might ask what is the thing that has made me make cakes and pastries and all those other things. Then I would say that one reason has been to give a concrete statement to my fantasy. In other words, instead of painting it, to make it touchable, to translate the eye into the fingers.

… making an object that is a concrete statement of visual perspective…

…What I am interested in is that the equivalent of my fantasy exists outside of me, and that I can, by imitating the subject, make a different kind of work from what has existed before."

—from THE STORE

Take I

She trails
drops of blood
give clues

to her journey
A disposable diaper
almost falling off

stuffed with white
powdery coke
Stylism

in the personal relationships
& the communications
between people

can seem implicative
of all else other than
relating naturally

if that's even possible
anymore

Take II *(Psyche rejects a fictive lover only she knows about)*

The contents
of your letter   I have so internalized
     as to create   a running conversation
          as I always do
     when I am caused again to look
               at you
          & consider
          your presence
in my emotional   and intellectual world

          I hear men
     in Morgantown, W.VA
     telling jokes of a sexual nature
               scandalous stories
     based on women who attracted them
     their wives look on stolidly

Will Petersen, the stone printmaker
    says he is most susceptible to fantasy
        & sexual attraction
    when his art has run out
        the need for a build-up
        from without, if not possible
        within

Once last summer, he continues—
    his work was so good
      the children were playing outside
      he got deep into the core
      of his perceptual self—
          was working well
          although there was still strong tension
              —would he lose it?

          Everything did not go right
        but still he was located
      there was a green all around,
      cows grazed inside himself

So I think
    when you demand someone who is
        trying artistically to figure things out
    in terms of mind/spirit/body the closeness
      of all these things

           to "be more earthy"
Go be that yourself!
    Take it somewhere else—it's you saying
    I need that right now
        as need for power in other affairs also

I don't forgive it
        The sexual is not always sacred, sometimes it
        should be delegated to a smaller place
The national obsession with the blowing
of one's nose, as Gurdjieff said

I can say all the following things:
        but once they are said you'll take off
        I'll be alone again
          the winter trees are so bare, skeletal
one must start all over again,
        building up a world to believe in

They are:
        I dig you
        I am obsessed with some form of you
        I would like to eat your body
        maybe someday there will be time
        and: I consider all this total
        regression
but I also like
        not having to worry if love has stopped
        having a man whose best interests are mine

There is a particular currency
       and exchange in these parts
  which however inflationary
is seeming to work very well ensuring
commercial satisfaction
for the members of this community

       (here Psyche's voice is lower)
      I saw myself this morning
         in the mirror

and knew that were I with a lover who
fixated on me as representative of the
continual passion in the outside world,
he would quickly be looking for another Helen
and I would be alone again

I would rather have
a very close good friend
of you   than you as lover

although I probably will continue
in my old woman fantasies of you
harmless as they are   because
they are delightful
and I am in
the habit

from

The Sun in Cancer

(1975)

The Minute-to-Minute Holding Company

i

It does seem to be a disaster
to be a woman in this time. I can't
triumph over the sense of frustration
that fills everything up I do.

I painted a table white & left it out after
darkness fell

it was wet
when I brought it in,
more wet
than when I painted it.
Things like that,
the fuckups of every day
rankle—
They're like the prosiness
which drives my head now,
inhabits this poem like stuffing,
all sparrows
no purple martins.

Maybe I don't put my house
high enough for birds to notice.
Maybe they're skipping this town.

I'm good and lost,
wandering in the woods looking for berries,
barricaded in an old house on the other side of
a door I can't keep closed, long hairy arms trying to get at
me, wondering how any woman

makes of her life more than
an elaborate minute-to-minute holding company,
more than a sham.
It's exhausting,
trying so hard every day/all day
to coordinate life
and accommodate it
to my proportions.
Others fuck around, screw each other,
live in the now and bask in their counter phobia.

I can't do anything like this.
My size is changing now,
I'm not comfortable.
Some days I seem to be pregnant and some days not,
how I look is everything now, a real attempt to *be*
a sexual object, since all the men I know are
taken anyway, with that. We all grew up in the same
era.

But there's no man
who's going to save me.
I don't have any sense of a sequined self
which will beckon
"the man I love"

One's alone with minimal conditions
with the prehensile organization
which co-ordinates the rest of the world,
a web among webs

I don't give a shit
about any man or any salvation
based on balling one man

& no family or friend relationship
is going to save me.
I'm alone
as any cow sitting under the trees
waiting patiently for what's next,
the brown blob
of her thoughts
looking out of blinking
fly-irritated eyes.

ii

I don't know what will come.
I wait, abhorring the passive,
and societal actions seem to arrange themselves
around me. He seems to be following me.
I'm following him, keeping too much track,
not laying my own track before me as I go.
I follow him because I've lost the leader of
myself. We move swiftly
& one concern runs out
before we have supplied the other, we don't know the speeds
we are running at until it's too late.
I would like to be able to manage my life,
not be led in circles by my thinking.

Yet always open
to the suggestive act:
the world loaded with
Christ & Buddha & your form
everywhere I look.
People write from England
extolling it's great at least one marriage seems intact

I jump, startled, & think,
the whole continent, the whole fucking continent
is afloat, we are swimming fast to
grab hold.

Prior Connections

Little wise fetus
you know so much
do you see spaces   colors
        pinks   shapes we've left out
not fitted into our gestalts

        the spaces are soon filled up
        with directive information

I half don't want you to emerge
& begin the process of losing
one by one, all you see inside
in order to get milk, warmth

            blocking out all these
            vast networks you've known
            simply because here,
            they don't summon from me
            what you now
                        need

String Sculpture of Barbara Hepworth

My concerns are round,
       abstract as the hole
puncturing space as through
       a capsule, spewing seeds from dried pod,
opening into
       wave, spiral, a tension of
vortices against which
       open space, the light we see,
is strung, defining more clearly
       enclosed energy and the shadows we work
within.

       As though I were to set up
multiple strings arching their proud backs
       at different lengths
from your involvement
       with space
on a grid of time
       to mine.
As though we would be able to record
       by these non-violent measures
the violence we did to one another
       & the grace we allowed to flower,
O so quietly,
       the sun moving across
the sky with the same quietness.   The strings
       hold their position, in analogous vastness.

This would be better than a camera,
       my first thought to record this dance,
because I would *make* the strings.

Like the sun, the strings don't record,
are part of
        progressive thought and action.
They would direct our attention
        like white swans,
focus our attention on action.

But how we did drift from these white
        markings, floating in a down of details
smothering our faces, how they
        consume us—humans do
get themselves down
        absolutely measured down
as though light were capable of
        no response, no discrimination,
simply of being captured in pigeon-hole boxes—
The subtle petty gunfire violence
        we do to our lives,
losing our hearts,
        spacing our heads into imprecise corners.

                    a prayer

Let us at least be
   free as the light coming before us,
open as the spaces stand before we enter.
Let us have the agility
to become these with good grace
Let us, if responsibility is
        the ability to respond
never indicate the Other
        is a passel of burdens,
reduce a human to the tiny boxes
        this civilized world packages everything in.

Let us squirm to free each other
        from boxes and our selves,
when we quarter our own spaces.

Let us not inhibit goldenrod,
        asparagus ferns,
the wind through the grasses;
        wind   space   time, let them
blow us up and out,
        free as we came to be when first-born

        And let the line then, and this love
be light
        as string, but let
the strings in their making
        not tie us tautly,
for surely we are more than our measurement.
        Surely we are more than our strings,
than our castings.
        And if we waver, if sometimes we seem
to be no more than
        the dance we make,
let us remember
        a white light and a blank space,
that the beauty of simply those
        made us want to speak.

The Second Pregnancy

—How are you today?
—I'm o.k.

> although my spine is breaking out in spots
> the snow that blanketed everything is filling up
>   the cavities in my stomach.
> the suicide on the window ledge is jumping
>   because she heard a man from below
>   call up,
>   "Jump! No one gives a damn!"

* * *

If I walked out into the clear white cold air there would be nothingness. Or a whole world of activity between the sewers and my feet: animals burrowed in tunnels, trees covered with snow until it sinks into warmer earth, brook running where it isn't frozen, animals scavenging for food, bearing the cold well because they have sturdy coats and yet holding their minds tight until some warmer energy comes to free them from this frozen world.

It's no longer possible to write about desire or frigidity or orgasm because the mind is tangled in the body's metabolism. So directed and subsumed by it, that the body is literally a feudal master over the mind. But their interplay is subtle and tenacious: they each tug on their pulley, making their weight felt, the nine months' pregnant body so insistent of its every condition, the mind so rebellious about controlling its land, its territory, its hopes and desires for the future. It lances on ahead like an outlaw in the new countryside sprung from a feudal barony where the master was impossible, and wages war on all the peasants he comes in contact with. On the loose, the mind would make a semblance of order but only has the distraught hay-strewn countryside to work with. His relations with everyone are thus discontinuous and outrageous in their obliquity.

Dream of the Collective

Important not to feel deluded, degraded
delighted, denuded or derided. Conspiracies
awaken. In the chest of drawers
is a snake rushing from hospital
to hospital, showing all the fangs
the family has. Somehow I was to
have the baby in a hospital in New York
I wasn't sure which one, was it Fifth
Avenue Flower or Beth Israel, my
mother-in-law was embarrassed; I asked
my father-in-law, my parents and doctors
were no where to be found,
& there was a hurry because I was in
transitional labor and subsequently on a plane,
in a taxi, in a traffic jam. There were
too many people in the streets and no way to
get around the individualism
sticking out from each person's body
like a radial pointed star's aura.

March Melting: Vermont

The mind
peculiar piece of living tissue
that it is, heads on into obscurity
dragging a piece of rope.
It sits down on the rope and begins
to chew it, valuing the children asleep
the tired back relaxing for a moment
which means the breasts too
relax
and begin to drip milk

The mind has learned a
great deal of information. All of it
is null/void
in the face of extreme exhaustion.
No one speaks
No one dares raise a hair's breath
      against the quiet of the afternoon,
      the sun shining on the insistent red-winged blackbirds
      who rise in a flurry to the tree,
      descend again in a vale
      all at once, forty black bodies, to
      the seeds on the snow.

A mind filled
with information.
Past history: past families, past people,
past places.
Past experiences collecting into nothing more
than the gestalt of present action,
blackbirds on the snow like atoms.

There is no minute
we are not in the present.
There is no way to live
other than in the present.

The continual drip
of the icicles
confirms this moment's
hold on time,
all else in the mind
unnecessary that does not
force to this realization.

There are no pussy-willows
near by
to bring inside.
Don't
they grow here?
Or is it that I have not looked?

Soft Walls

One now, a lean male one
has lost
a sense of the world,
is institutionalized.
He doesn't any longer want to get out.
I am like that about the house.
I must be afraid of the world.
I must be afraid I will eat the world
or the world will eat me.

There are walls
but people say the walls are spongy.
You can walk through them,
move through them like a monkey letting
breezes move through his trees, if you even try.
I am so afraid of the consequences
that I don't try
but I watch the world going on outside
and wonder,
where is it and why am I not in the world?

Most of the old people around me
are also prisoners in their houses,
perhaps not of their own choice.
But I'm only thirty, and they are seventy.

Presumably they did a lot of things once.
Perhaps they went out to see their children,
just newly married, set up on their own farm.
Perhaps they had a farm themselves
in their day (this is not their day, they say)
rather than a house in the village

and they went to their cows
and their cows came to them.

It is all a matter of degree,
I know that.
I would like to try to walk through the walls.
I wonder if they really are
soft and malleable
or hard, as I usually think of them.
I wonder if they will scrape my skin as
I pass through, or if it will be a smooth passage,
Death's mirror pulling Orpheus.

Last night a student came over
from the world
His mind was falling apart—perhaps he was high.
He called my husband a shit over and over
and sat in the living room cursing at him,
talking in great abstractions at break-neck pace
about the Kabbalah, superimposing on Richard the
face of the father he hates, who is
flying now to the hospital to see him.
Schizophrenia. The mind starts replicating
cells which can't fit into the existing system,
which ravage and plow under the patterns of hate
and hostility until they bubble up
like an autumn fountain in Venice.

I don't know where it puts us,
any of us in our larger or smaller worlds.
Molly Miranda lies on the floor,
her five-months-old toes in her mouth,
smiling and laughing because she's not
hungry or wet or sleepy.
The infinite sadness of all sentient beings.

Starting the Seeds

Again, indoors.
This enormous
Commitment
To very probable failure,
As though the will wanted to
Involute again, to see the skin
It had forgotten the stripes of.

But angels
Don't decide
Do they have the time,
Energy,
Will,
To guard our sheep this year
To speak through our mouths,
To try our troubled minds
With their composites

The seeds finally push up
On a blowy April peeking-through-soil
Cold day,
Hardly together do we have
Ourselves.

But we don't know how
To stop the show.
We're glad of that.
Blessed ignorance
To shuffle on
forward, arms swinging
and singing,
There, and back again.

The Bargain

Don't be afraid. Go at your fear at a run, hands up,
be a pitching two-masted ship
tack first north, then south, gain purchase
on the sea, go *at* the wave with one great burst.

If you are afraid in day travel by day, meeting the bandit sun
and tussling with his robber sunbeams
They will want to rob you of all the strength you have.

The planets, disinterested and dependent on the sun,
won't help.
In the end you'll die like cinquefoil
and in the whole set of the species
it won't have come to much,
a good life,
a good death,
rain in a cycle of rain

Your friends
will reveal themselves
as others of the same species
focused on their own
wants, needs, desires,
if you talk in a way they can understand
you will block out the voice that keeps you
moving
beyond your circle
into the world.

The Sun in Cancer

My work and my garden grow.

Abstracted from every one,
tending to small things:
chipmunk, line of swan, crest of
yellow warbler.

The pull of the nursing mouth
on my breast—deep, streaming.

In this way the connectives
are left out
to all but me,
and tunnel
I do deep down
where it is safe,
like other women crawl into bed
alone, reading until they put the light out,
the night outside so rich
so fragrant, so full of new spring—

Are there other places I can live
where there will not be a question
after every tiny sprig planted?

Where my father's baked powdery bones
sifting through my fingers
will not be irrelevant?

We have to let more people in.
Perfection in situations is not

to be strived at but rather
a livability,
a lack of stress that makes
four people happy, not just myself.

Dandelions in high grass blow in the wind,
not remembering my father's indiscretions,
my mother's stoic pride.
Something other than dignity
makes the ferns unfurl.

Letter to My Mother from Northwood Campus

> *By being touched, moved, and opened by the*
> *experiences of the soul, one discovers that what*
> *goes on in the soul is not only interesting and*
> *acceptable, but that it is attractive, lovable and*
> *beautiful.*
>
> —James Hillman, *The Myth of Analysis*

1.

Dear Lady! It is not in how beautiful
our patina is, whether our shoes are shined
whether the nose is runny or the face washed
or whether these people are beautiful or ugly.

People are dropping dead in India now
and Sylvia Porter continues to discuss
how Americans will move up, class by class.
When you were young
you must have had the drive
not to scuttle your fears
underneath plants, underneath
the new abstract painting,
all the back roads must have
beckoned once, as they do
now for me.

I look over at your wig,
which you don't mind getting wet.
Could you have cancer?
My jacket needs to go to the cleaners,

and we argue about that.
If I sent everything to the cleaners
you want me to
there would be no time
to find sparrow nests
to watch the fog lift from the Winooski

To watch the sparrow find food
as the dead drop in India.

Those dead are not far from
my thoughts, even though our pancakes
taste good. I'm not for a minute
fooled by this luxury
you've brought.
It'll be gone when you leave.
My cat doesn't have the ease
to enjoy being inside
without his bowels turning to water.
Most of our differences come down
to ease: what we have sacrificed
to find it or dodge it.
Most of what occupies me
you don't find pleasurable,
the concept of *a work*
is hard to explain, though
you are painting now.

The ways of the soul are dark ladies
I follow them through the trees,
they wend through pitch pine, the secondary
growth which replaced white pine in Vermont,
a foursome of habited nuns who spawn
blessed occurrences in every corner of

the natural world. I seek men
who work with stone, who work with wood
and words, but I try not to glorify them.

Women I love
are falling along the road, prisoners in their houses,
vulnerable—the central government,
deluded as empire always is, refuses to help.
These women join my proud dark ladies and
pull me along, we walk around the ponds naming
beech, birch, oak, and maple
their faces become the trees, they sing softly,
October drizzle matting their leafy
faces, silent to anyone who is moving so fast.

2.

Dear lady of the nights growing old,
I may have glowered,
a poppy shrinking into a teardrop.
You pronounce me erratic.
Why, you ask, do you dangle
from the streetlamps
and yet march in submarine procession
to a rhythm of oppression?
Where is the consistency here?

I answer: The painting of a map of Plainfield
has the town's dirt mixed with pigment.
Because I'm young
I'm not bitter.
If I lose my way
it is because the bats

lost their sonar
before I was born.
The crown prince misplaced his jewels,
his fiancée, his map
of the new world. I wait
for a bus that comes
only when I watch very hard
the fire that licks Eros'
golden fingernails.
Wooden church steeples
topple into the sacristy at these occasions,
the local people watch with confusion,
but the dead still line up along the road.
They can't hold their meetings
in the new Knights of Columbus hall.

Sunsets err also.

I can't move any faster
than the heaviest, most unhappy lady
berating her child
at the five-and-ten checkout counter;
my fate is tied to hers
the sap in my veins rises as she yells at
him. *You have the most beautiful child*,
I say, walking past her.

I think of following them home,
rescuing the boy

3.

In the history of psychology,
Psyche at one point became mind,
and mind became brain, and head
became equated with soul.
All that leaves out where I spend
my nights of terror, a rationalism
I no longer live with,
a shadowy husband you assume I'm married to,
but who I left long ago.
I'm set up in different quarters now.
When I talk, pigeons
walk into my plate; I eat sugar-laden leaves—
you and I aren't sharing enough assumptions.
We speak of daily terrors
trying to find where the soul lives;
the waterfalls where the soul swims free.

My dark ladies
live in a cemetery of leaves
the wind blows through.
Look there!   Glimpses of death, other voices,
fast-moving shades.
Will they take me in when I die?
And you too?

Work out your salvation with diligence,
as Buddha said,
and don't be surprised
by anything except the beauty
& ugliness you have not internalized.

The Delius Cycle

I want to sing
high-pitched like
a seal in the night
after Delius has gone home,

far away comes the sound,
ringing in his ears as he
makes his quiet preparations
for bed in his cold flat,
soft snow sifting
in the streets of Cracow.
Go back, young man
says the voice of the seal,
Delius knowing he can't
go back to England or any of his life
before this minute,
that he's in the propeller of a plane
only climbing higher
cloud over cloud,
lifting itself up by catching
the far-rushing wind
underneath its wing span.

Far below, a little boy flying a kite,
thinks of his kite's crossbow fleetingly
as he runs as fast as he can pell-mell
down a rocky hill, catches a glimpse of the
plane above and thinks of its wings:
that they are similar to his kite's width,
he can't see Delius

mashed up in the propeller, his body dangling
hanging bone by bone,
dragged through a vapory sky.

ii

A man and a woman talk, sitting in their living room,
all they have made around them. In the bookcases,
all their books. At a friend's, the children they
created together. They talk of their life, trying
to build sentences, though they barely can,
letting words flow out of their mouths
like molten aluminum, letting these words frame up
the meaning of their life together. They try
to ascertain what their life is as a couple.
The words circle and bind each into separate
and conflicting stories.
They try to corral some essence of their marriage
by endlessly telling
these stories in new words, putting new value on different
situations they have brought into their life.
They use too many words—it becomes complicated
and heated, who they are to one other
becomes devalued, obscured as a foggy road.
The words are dangerous; they take on
a life of their own, become javelins and swords thrown
too easily. The words charge up, rushing,
they hurt themselves and each other badly.

In their heart of hearts, they want this to stop.
It seems separate from themselves,
like a war waged far away, but of course
they are causing it, making it happen.

They want to be flowing around the house
as they were earlier, circulating around each other
and the children—happy, amusing themselves, and call *that*
the life. But here they are, stuck like darts in a corkboard
in sentences with canons and epochs of syntax.
Finally they admit the words have utterly confused
and confounded them. As their rage deepens
they begin uttering threats with finality,
hurling devastating sentences which pummel the other
like repeated blows to the head.
They lose the meaning of words, dangerous
since they are writers and words are their tools all day.

They know that words are sacred, they might as well be hurling
the body and blood of Christ at
one another. Words sustain them. Were each to start a new life
with different partners, they would eventually be using the
words of affection they give to one another like gentle offerings,
simply in different living rooms.

Realizing this, they stop talking.
They declare themselves unfit for words.
They will only show love
through physical movement. It's not important
who made the first move. They make love—
a deep pervasive warmth flows from each of seven chakras
heating the other. They flood each other
with warmth. Afterwards, the man makes a fire and drives up
the snowy hill to retrieve the children; the woman makes
dinner and a dessert. They are considerate in their actions
about the house, trying wordlessly to make it comfy and
cozy for one another. They save themselves by distancing
themselves from hurtful words, using none
except of calm, slow feeling. Soundless.

The action of emptying the trash if done correctly.
The action of sifting out what is of use.
The action of determining if anything is of use.
The action of taking first one very small step,
letting go, of taking another, seeing if that works,
of falling back with a bump if it doesn't work.
The action of walking, once one can take a few steps.
The action of believing one can walk
only comes after one has shown oneself
step follows step.
Feet go one/right/after/another.

Robby learned to skip today.
He skips everywhere now.
To find the clues, he skips.
He first did it two hops on a foot at a time,
then when I did it for him, he watched carefully,
and did it: a hop on one foot, then a step that's
a hop on the other. That is skipping.

Miranda is learning to walk
and Robby is learning to skip.
The complication of the one to the other
is exactly the difference of five years.

iv

The name of the game is love
or power, or
impeccability. Or
integrity. No one knows

what any of those terms mean.
Good taste is variable,
what is good taste to one and
totally necessary is
anathema to another.

I came downstairs and opened the
curtains. There was a certain amount
of good taste there, and respect,
it was an act not of daring but
common sense. We want just
enough madness to open ourselves
up, but suicide is not an alternative.
Depression and anxiety will always be with us.
Writing is not shimmying up trees.
Writing is not what you think.
The internal dialogue is a frenzied rat in a maze,
haphazard in its endless attempts at satisfaction.

The Eleventh-Hour Edge

The quiet face quickens.
The face at the door, malgré all intent,
malgré all human plans
quickens the blood, a rush
to the face.

I react to the work
only after having responded
to the person, but still I am
not totally a humanist.

Our commitment is to the world
of things: meaning systems,
meaning how animals deck themselves out,
to find food and mate and stay alive.

No one seems to be able to
figure anything out
without it going through a mind.
If I learn about social systems
or the herring gull's world
it is not so much a love of birds
but of comprehending
what birds do.

Do you know about larches:
those brilliant Halloween trees
which stand totally unrevealed
until the last minute before the frost,
an eleventh hour conifer

                    Time so precious,
so jammed up because leaves will fall
the swan song of larches, orange-yellow
before the hard frost hits.

Trees at Grossinger's

The height of stately Catskill pine trees,
trees which watched this hotel grow,
trees which knew the original building,
    its verandah all around the outside of the first floor,
trees which watched
        cars replace buggies and
        change, through the '20s, '30s, '40s, until
        cars look like what Robby cuts out, glossy color
        photos of long shiny luxurious
        apartments riding on 400-million-year-old oil;

Trees which smiled at
        babies running where this house now stands,
heard babies cry heard
        family arguments rise and fall until
the children, grown, came to regard
        decisions as important and if not binding
        imperative,
came to decide not to be here, not to
        man the hotel,
to identify with other evergreens—

Trees which
        few look carefully at,
trees with deep roots which
        when surface, look like stone,

Trees much older than me
will outlast us, as they've outlasted Jennie
and her husband Harry and the woman who ran the
women's locker room—they will outlast all of us.

Green shimmering in afternoon sun!
Trees which I could never paint,
even with color awareness and color shading;
these trees will persist through snow and wind
           long after I'm hundreds of miles away
           looking out at the strength of sugar maples
           and paper birches
           against the wind & snow
           winter will hurl soon in Vermont;

Trees purchased in 1919 as part of the Nicolas Farm
           by Jennie not far from Ahavath Israel where
           she is buried

Trees which seem so incredibly strong
           so full of integrity
           harming no one, no man
           and yet dependent on man's good will,
which could chop them down in a moment's rash decision
           of "improvements," meaning golf courses

Trees I worry about you,
           because many of the plans around here
           seem shortsighted and destructive

Trees which in my female, motherly, over-developed
           empathy and altruism
I can no more save
           than I can myself.

Back Road to Barre

I take the back roads everywhere now because
I want to prove to myself that I am wedded to
Vermont and all its difficulty   I am not
expecting ease or for a minute dependent on ease
and am totally patient with the hardest life
situations even though I am not in the heat of
any moments that would totally undo me
except of my own making   men and women
can do what they want
although they will suffer immeasurably for their vision

When I follow them out and they come out where
they are supposed to it is a victory to me   I
even don't mind seeing the young boys dressed
in red checkers proud of their guns totally intent
on the kill in the middle October drizzle, I like
seeing the men going to work wedded to the harshness
of whatever their job is, it is pretty difficult I am
one with them in the urgency to not live in a manner

that would indicate there is any ease whatsoever
or that this country has any ease because whatever ease I
have seen has been purchased at such great cost to the
other inhabitants who have been blocked out of the mind
intent on ease, at others' expense—and although others
probably say of me she is living an easy life not for
one minute does my manner indicate so to any who know me
and that is perhaps the greatest kindness I can offer.

Sea Poppies

So many times
you blasted
      from your full egoism,
trod heavily on top of,
what I considered lovely and sacred—

I stopped, always,
         with amazement
and later understood
         I must have sought you out
for that,
     to force me to re-embrace
more tightly
     the precious,
beautiful, and
        yes, even
            sacred.

Dealing

Robby: I will give you a kiss
            if you give me a bowl of cereal
Lindy: I will give you a bowl of cereal
            if you will let me wash your face
Robby: I will let you wash my face
            if you will read me a Narnia chapter
Lindy: I will read you a Narnia chapter
            if you will get into your jammies
Robby: You can spell those (gesturing to names
            Duchamps, Satie and Cage) with my letters
            on the ice box
            if you will put them back in their alphabet

Lindy: You can exorcise out the spirit in my life
            if I can enjoy the sweet look on your face.

Animus

Beautiful
and most beautiful
and then again beautiful.
We are the masters
of the transcontinental railroad.
Spies
        applaud in the night:
peeking out from the
tattered curtains, they
watch our doings.
We say the right things
at the right times.
They circle to get on top
of us, a suitable
position from which
to best us,
and then leave, filing out
into the 30° below night.

We don't say
a word to one another.
We know we partake heavily
of each others' mystery.
Were we to use one another
fully we would
use up our time here,
burn out a survival candle
that must last for years.
We don't want to start
the wreck of the world
the eclipse of the sunrise

and so all our motions
are elaborately under-extended,
a shyness belies our ages,
as it settles into rigidity, circumspection.

You are so archly silent, so evenly tongue-
tied, as am I.
When I write about you
it's an anthropomorphism
making the night, the stars, the cold
       the bone cold we're growing fond of,
into a person. It's almost like constantly
writing about myself,
an egocentrism
sees no further
than one's own breath.

The river flowing
underneath the ice
combats this.

Creating another life
might combat this,
if it was handled skillfully.

Being more privy to the spies
of knowledge
than emotion
might combat this.

It is symptomatic of
a human relational problem,
of what is sexuality,
what is the boundary of friendship, the

nuclear family,
that I still involve myself
with the question of you.
I want
marriage with everyone,
a family bigger than two parents and two children,
no affairs, deep friendship.
I refuse to accept the world's definition of
what means most to me, in any way.
But you're the main person
I would people my walls with.
The referent my mind dreams up
in its habit of identification.

A View of the Stone

for Peter Ruddick, sculptor

In the stone is movement
particles changing & dissolving,
creating themselves into new structures
As much as we have to be aware of our words
& hear the other that puts them into our heads,
you have to be aware of that energy speaking to you
from the stone, fight
not to drown it out in
your own speaking, your own mind's talk

Thus there is no stasis
in the piece you look at
Bring your self and your body's torque
to its grid of play,
& leave refreshed or used up by the contact
it takes your lust into it and makes something
better with it than you could have made alone,
dancing in the streets
of your alone-soul

Your mind though exhausted should only become
strong
by learning the stone's tensions & balances
so much greater than yours!
You and the stone *become* beauty
torque to others because you've
fellated each other: others listen now
you're the bridge between the stone's talk
and the world

Picking up the stone
putting it into the truck
lugging it around
it's speaking not our words
but continually moving a graceful waltz inside itself
in the same way I move within myself
while we are talking nonsense to each other
in a totally suggestive way
We hide behind our talk, it keeps us from action.
The contact with the stone is cleaner—
words not an option.

None of these meetings are impossibilities
but we have to listen carefully
to get the right responses
not jump the gun & shoot the stone or each other
or drown out the silent speech
in a voice-over of words

This, like everything else at
the core of our lives is,
sadly, if we are unable,
a matter of belief

The Changeling

It's hard for me to be patient
and wait my time.
Leaves curl red into my hand,
caterpillars change from furry to velvet
within my palm.
That is a stimulation we used to play
into each others' palm with our fingers,
lightly grazing the inside of your excitement
like a bare toe flirting underneath a table
with an unaware leg.
We still tickle
in different ways—
we are more sophisticated,
we throw ourselves
over the cliffs & fly

The world gently changes.
It is changing all the time
if only I look, I can see it.
Whenever I have looked, it has been there to watch,
a different child put there by fairies, complicated
if I could to see it.

Your time will come, the world bubbles
to the river pulsing inside me, which hears,
knows how to wait. I look out
the window at children playing,
glad I'm not chasing the red ball across the street,
glad I'm not fantasizing about a toy,
or the next birthday.

I fantasize about changing.
I dream about being the changeling the world is.

I like my age that waits for arms to reach down
and enfold me. I like my age, the way it dashes against
ocean spumes of whale breath shot high

The gaps I can't put together now
will be gathered up. I feel about my younger despairs
like the girl speaking of the insane asylum today:
it is necessary to get one's trip together if only
to prevent ever being *here* again.

Each year the body has revealed more.
Each year the plan has been more coherent.
Each year I have lost
and found myself just in time.

New Morning

A morning like all the others.
The great dogs
range over the hill.
The thump on the porch announces they
are here, eating the cat's food.
Infuriatingly large and immoral, trampling over
all we have, carrying away
a broken piece of a blue dish they smashed.

I detest the dogs.
In my virulence is all the distaste
I have for this place, where a cultivated disorderliness
lives in the inhabitants' eyes.
People here are cruel,
have a real mean streak,
mean talkin', mean actin.'
One is rammed up among so few
with one's insistent needs,
running breathlessly
in their own Purgatories. They can't be
anything but selfish and cruel.

Marriage is like
the small town, the inhabitants are self-sufficient
screened off from one another, amazed
that no one's home
But no matter how imperfect you are,
I would rather be
with you & let the rest of the world go hang.

One seeks in the eyes of the other,
restitution, a solution for one's own
soul-sickness. The
town will not do, the human is *polis*,
not to seek
cure in another
but in one's own revitalization.

I have known that for years.
But in the haste to build a perfect union,
built a superstructure of dependency.
It is a quiet thought,
        comes while sewing.
Sadly, my actions, the desperation
        of my energies come out of the old model,
do not accord.

What I Know

This is a story that admits of no essence larger than the
        human.
This is a story that sees only the solar system, although the
        whole galaxy is known to be extant.

A girl grows up
pinning her every heart's beat
on her father, her mother the enemy
always exacting requirements of good behavior

As she gets older she perceives parts of herself
are like her mother; she studies with fear of failure
in college alone with fear that she will do things wrong
she cannot rip her mother from the parts of her body
she hates, but wants to love.

She begins to fall "in love"
with men who desire
her crystalline body,
her ability to build them up
and make them feel powerful,
her laughter & gaiety & lack of selfishness.

The main thing she has learned so far is how to make others
happy, not herself
a spirit of generosity that allows her
to talk better about another's troubles than her own.

She confuses her own worth
    with the love men give her.
One after another she adores,

worships, they seem so brilliant
so much a part of the world

They love her because
she pleases them
goes away when she should
and makes them feel good.

Gradually she dimly perceives
that her life
has been a pattern of seeming rights
with the wrongs only obvious to herself

>   when she tries to explain these things to her mother
>   & her sisters
>   they suggest that she leave the expensive college
>   & transfer to the State University close to home
>   if she is really that ungrateful

During a summer at a newspaper
she spins into a love affair
with an older married man
in time he begins to seem corrupt
He comes down hard on closet fags in the government
the ad agency which seemed glamorous from Denver
seems shabby now that he's in New York
with his cigar and new clothes
he seems sad and middle-class

She runs in a stark terror
& marries a man she has loved,
has kept communicating with through other love affairs.
Sometimes they have to work hard
to strike any kind of match

She learns a whole new life
her worth apart from her sexuality
is important for the first time;
she works hard, reading, learning, writing
until again
            each day
she begins to feel she is running,
out of breath,
                trying to be bright enough
                read   write   enough
                to not be emotional but articulate
                    logical and conceptual
She has to fight for survival
  in a world where she's hardly learned the terms
She yearns to make this new world *just hers*
where she will have to live up to   nothing

                    what is obscure is whether the world
                        is really like this
                    or whether she exacts this pressure
                        from herself

They live in different places
make a family   believe in ideals
(peace and contentment)
help one another when each is down

Most of the time
what they have is to her a noble experiment
        she totally believes in
but sometimes the whole horror
        of her early years comes back
        (he battles similar early ghosts

& she feels like a nubbin
        wanting only the paternal affection
of a man she can please who will
        take care of her, shield her
from all she is scared of

She rejects her husband in her mind
in these moments
        as everything she must live up to
She feels incapable of ever pleasing him or
        herself
and begins to slide downhill,
confusing mother husband lovers father

                Because life goes on
she meets a man
who after seven years of marriage is the first
entity to excite her admiration & imagination
He is resident in their world
& brings out in her
earlier reactions towards a type of man
        she admired and desired in a steady pattern, for years

He is either the great force in her life,
the great love
or a neurotic distraction from solving these problems.

The ultimate question
whisks away when stars,
hurricanes, natural forces are mentioned:

whether there *are* Great Loves
or whether humans when they mature
stop such thinking
                & concentrate on business,

On helping each person in the family
On spiritual awareness and the growth of consciousness
given how difficult life is
for even the four-year-old

Believing in family
she conceives a second child
although her husband is unsure it's wise

This is seen by the new man
(however flippantly said) as armor
to protect herself from finding the aggression
to be with him.

The months which follow
are a difficult time.
When she is physiologically sick
she is confused psychologically
& yet as the pregnancy progresses she finds
the new child
reason enough
to be clear on these things
So she pursues them doggedly
as others pursue endangered species

When she is most embattled
against the various parts of herself
most faint
in the image she makes in the world
the man becomes all-important & seems to be
a shadow of the only self
she has really known   the old self
of childhood & narcissism which was "unselfish"

She talks to him in the old way
    endlessly leads him out
    so he is telling her his whole life
She sets an elaborate trap for him
     & he feels chased, but since he is lonely
        he responds

When she is with him
for long periods of time
there is not enough between them

but when she's not seen him
for a long time
the shadow builds in strength & visage
By the time they come together,
it is too charged, she is too intense

Her own powers against this force
seem to wane
       & she is heavily weighted down,
        sullen & depressed & obnoxious,
lusting   after a life
she has known only as child
which is gone

Again and again she falls into these vistas
& is pulled out by the least
     intellectual concentration
     on any one thing

Gradually she sees she is motivated
to make work
strong and hungry for knowledge

She finds relief
        in the constructions of thought
        in mastering difficult material

The matrices
    take the pressure off any relationships
to decide who she loves
        who she is attracted to
        whether she is attractive to X
        whether she feels responsive to her husband

She learns how to survive
      in this new way
& begins to value the connections
she makes
      between different ways of
      perceiving phenomena

She comes to see she is One
         who can watch inside & outside
         with equal insight & pleasure
She begins to feel worthwhile
& churns out great batches of material
based on moving forward
She participates more in the world

Still, every day
she fights   to keep her balance
  between these early horrors, easy regressions
      & her present growth

The sun shines
Vermont wind blows unseasonably warm in December
     the comet is coming & they worry about California

Yet inside, she's excited   the growing child coming along,
    she finds peacefulness
at having work to rely on and
having worked through
so much of this

Upper Road

Is it called Barre Hill Road?
> That incredible arch down
>> the whole town laid out
>> flat in your palm
>>> incredible
>>> it takes your breath away

What is it about
> Vermont towns
> from above!
> You are always wanting to
>> climb the surrounding hills
> Because you know
> it'll look amazing to see down

Misty, as far as the eye can see
> the whole valley laid out
> smooth as your palm

The Road to Judy Farnham's Daycare

Oh
little creature-culture
Oh
little animal garden
can you make the transition
from our village house
where we are whirring around in
a vortex of boundaries & ideas
to her animal rolling hills
where everything sprawls & bawls
& you are piling over hill & dale?

O little Mohawk
you probably have it in hand
better than I
but there's a seer here
who's given me three words
I hoe by:

    tender
    self-absolving
    rutabagas.

This World Is Not My Home

Sheathed like a slim foot
in this special beautiful shoe of
on the brink, the necessity of being always
able to produce good work
making in me a taut tension so that

>   the lassitude other men & women
>   allow themselves are no longer possible,
>   condition of being always about to explode

into a thousand slivers of glass
or an honest man's hand

>   steam rising into billowing clouds
>   from Vermont Yankee, her 90 cows
>   graze placidly, their milk laced with radioactivity
>   of which she does not have clear *proof*
>   "Ya gotta admit it's kinda pretty,"
>   she says, "on a sparkling clear day the steam billowing
>   up in all those vapory clouds out across the river ..."

O Connecticut River of waters cooling evil
underwater currents in a river of madness
tritium-contaminated groundwater
killing fish and the whole Chain of Being

>   For all of us: the abstraction the life,
>   the work deals with promotes
>   this necessity of sure hits,
>   a pressure to hit the target fast
>   the next action unimportant unless
>   laced with risk & the possibility of destruction

Still, I have stayed alive
these thirty years,
and so has she and he and she
but at what cost to others?

O *don't you think*
we should spend a long time together
            I sd, knowing I cd go off the road,
            children in the car, any moment &
            increasing my chances by seeking him out;
            no time is propitious for the end of the world

I see how people entwine
            themselves in calamitous events,
            Malgré their intentions,
            their sense of orderliness;

It's one thing to play tennis
aggressively in the morning sunlight
the ball touching splintered keystones of inquiry
            another to say, I will come
            & carry you off someday

                        We can't make it anymore
in an orderly fashion,
the ideas cloud the waves coming in,
sands absorb a cycle of the same water

                        Lawrence pacing the porch of his
                        beachfront cottage outside Sydney
                        writing *Kangaroo,* sun in the waves
                        wondering what man is coming to—
                        what he himself should be doing.
                        Working every morning,
                        working every morning.

from

Outlands & Inlands

The Easy Life

There was a smoothie had a flat tire asked a studying law
student in a near-by apartment if he could use the phone
got the tire fixed asked the student if he'd like to
go for a drive to have a drink they do they drive into
the south of France visit relatives the law student has
liked since childhood
The smoothie shows him up the uncle becomes somehow
coarse and vulgar the niece who has always admired the
young law student sees how bumbling & awkward he is next
to the smoothie who flatters & charms her
on the way back after this long day after they stop
here and there for a few drinks the smoothie who is
driving too fast drives off a cliff escapes unharmed
the young law student is killed who had earlier that
morning been studying in the sunlight for his bar
exams
the smoothie tells the police sadly that he
doesn't even know his name, oddly enough
& it is sad because he too feels by this time very
close to the student
not to mention us, the audience who have become
completely involved in the student's life nostalgia
memories self-confidence future plans.

Home Again

Delight (though there is absolutely
Nothing
To look forward to)
To come home

     Because we can't get a start
     Anywhere but here.
     As snows stop, wind says
     Okay. Enough for this far north country
     And goes off to Greenland,

To try someone else's patience.

     We rest,
     Become cotyledon.
     We can only move forward
     By the year nudging us there,
     Us, we would squat in the same old corner
     Mourn old shoes,
     Lost songs;
     Peripatetic visionaries
     Who move because the months nose us on.
     Still, March is ending.
     Still, it takes April to make
     Spring viable, grab as ice did &
     Last interminably; for sap to drip
     Only when the weather turns
     Do we allow ourselves the calm
     With coffee on the porch in the sun, to say
     We might be happy together.

The Quiet Ones

Speak
To the trees.
They know you better.
They're not going to
Let on; the silence,
The non-activity of spangled tears
Isn't what they see.

They've got it together:
A wind, a light snow,
A swamp underneath that never dries up
When everything else
Needs to be watered

They are climbing towards
That launching pad
High in the sky,
They don't think
Of constantly starting over again.
They have patience, the slow burn of
Augustus—to wait it out.

Blue daisies in the field
Consider them friends.
They don't
Constantly have to stop
To tie a shoelace.

The Poet's Métier

What is my—
what you call it
my—
what can be described,
as, this poet
does this,
& this one, this.

I'm a cat on a fence.
The fire horn blows.
Those who live around here
can tell where the fire is from listening.
Just like I'm not here,
geographically, never really
settled in here—
There's a skittering between my eyelids,
a sort of imbalance
only righted by walking
very carefully along the fence,
& then down another,
and another.

I cover whole cities that way,
fence by fence,
never touching wooden back porches,
never having to cross backyards,
so light in my cat step
I leave no tracks.

But I never know
where the fire is,

& my poetry to others
& my self
is not easily classified.

Is that a fatal weakness?
Does it mean that its
not really *on,*
like it engages me
but no one else?

If I wear a long magenta skirt
& a complex necklace
high button black boots
push my long brown hair behind my ears
with a quick flick of my hand so my face
can be seen better,
will I put it over—
& no one will notice?

Instead of spending $48 on groceries,
could I buy myself
some really far out clothes?

I'd rather be a cat,
walking successive winding fences,
silent
& moonstruck.

Aware of One Another a Thousand Dogs Bark

Nothing that comes or goes is free. Is home free. Tastes like chunks of black coal in the mouth, a horrible taste, coffee warmed up too many times in your mouth, the taste of a good thing gone bad.

He and she and perhaps all of them all in the human race although they did not say it, did not dine it in their daily bread or ask it to tea, were attracted to people under their thumb. Who could not get the best of them: the others stuck up like rocks in the path of roaring water, to be gotten around, to be mowed down or smashed over somehow, perhaps only in the fury and force of the pounding. As she watched she could not help participating, simply having been born and some mother having put hours of time into making a viable position for her in the world meant that she was out there with the rest, struggling and biting and sighting the horizon for those who would block her progress and those who would help it.

Who could not get the best of one. Who could not best one. Love and war, competition, the daily market, IBM, it is up. It is down. Someone loses from another winning. Success is finding those who you like, who you're on some equal footing with, a bank or a hill together, a semblance of definitions in common between you two.

The birds sang, singing in their way, concerned with their business, whatever it was. Not making an effort or having the ability to understand or even care about human competition. Which did not work the other way around, humans did feel responsible for understanding bird-paths. & yet they were singing wholes, not parts, serene and frantic in their arts, unconnected, unconcerned with human competition. Which tried its best to subvert itself. Counter to this trend ran a humanizing loving trend, six individuals living together in an Ann Arbor town house, really trying to lose images and love each other enough to make something beautiful. Although we hear about it only, never travel to Jerusalem to see it for ourselves, does it work? This is the Crusade. We want it to work. We want to spend our time well, lose our competitiveness, make some money, sell our house. We want to be born.

The Woman Who Thought of Herself as a Girl

Take I

She was limited, but not alone because of her children. She had been limited as a child, a teen-ager, a young lady. Now she was limited as a stunted woman, roped into a cycle of too much Thorazine and in and out of Maine State Hospital, but still, as she said to everyone, she was not yet a freak.

She dwelt in the house of ordinariness. Her house was as difficult to live in as the hospital, it was clear; the one was respite from the other, but each had its own craziness. Never had there been piping in the sounds of a world of richness and calm, but only incessant demand. Before the children, it was the demand to produce the children. When they were babies, it was all right; there were enough images in her head about babies to make that condition tolerable. But as they grew older, their specific selves took on form and their needs nudged into demands. She could see the hydra-head she had produced getting out of hand. She was a creek run dry. When she lifted one heavy foot before the other, small eddies of sand sifted down into her empty footprints.

She guessed she had not brought the separate things in her life together sufficiently tight to form a mesh. She felt herself drifting out through the large loopholes in her life's existence as the television blared. When she chatted with a neighbor, the sameness of life she had always known waved into focus and reassured her, but even as she walked back into the house she heard the dull roar which preceded panic. She judged she might get to the kitchen table before it overtook her, and wondered what the road outside would look like then.

When Melinda saw her taking her slow walk each day, sometimes she went to the road and walked with her, just for the company. Melinda listened to her talk. It was much the same as the other neighbor women's, except nicer; less catty. It seemed for all of them the world resided in units of sameness. The same material was gone over again and again: the town, what to buy, what cost a lot now, what one had bought at the Giant Discount Store. When the husbands went to Guards for the weekend the weekend blended into the weekdays. People were pretty much the same except that some were rowdier, some more shiftless and therefore had less means, men had most to do outside. Inside was mainly TV. There was not much to learn, rather a right way to do things (having to do with neatness and orderliness) and a wrong way.

The woman who thought of herself as a girl knew the neighbors thought she was crazy. She was embarrassed about the hospital, that she had to go there. But her house was as neat as anyone's, wasn't it? And she certainly stayed home. She didn't run around, as some of them did. No matter what happened, she would stay home, as long as her children needed her.

Take II

Green leaves are proper. Not brown leaves, which must be burned; black leaves are dirty. Deep loam, compost, bacteria, are all dirt, and therefore dirty. You must wash your hands. You will probably get infected. The green quatrain will fill up. Retarded, the loops the turtle can swim through are quite big! He can get out. But no knowledge grows on the sides of his aquarium because there is no space, money, joy, just sameness and an artificial light-bulb.

Some fish are rowdy and some poor. Some don't watch out for themselves or try. What can you do with a man just won't try? Or a fish, for that matter. Because we keep everything so clean, we look to have more money than we do. & because we don't look the least bit different (See how our jade lawn reflects our lovely eyes! See how our clean white driveway shows what soft white arms we have!) we look the same as everyone, we won't be singled out, no you could never say we weren't *all right* in the total eyes of collective Amerika. Everyone is looking at us all the time.

To the Cape Elizabeth Ladies

> *reading* From the Wonderful Folks Who
> Brought You Pearl Harbor *to one another*

April 15, 1972

Daytime doldrums.
Knitting.
           Making loops.
Making daily sense.
               or non-sense.
Loose freedom of bodily activity
missing here. We're rigid in chairs.
Not to move is the object, as in school.
This book club is like the first years of school,
       show & tell, where you don't have to be
       responsible or really *know* anything
you just tune in & listen, if you dig,
& run your mind if you
don't

Rob plays freely, lining up trucks & cars
on the lower shelves. Michael huddles in the corner
with his blanket and thumb, daunted by the stern glances
from his mother, who is herself uncomfortable.
I write freely.
We are tantalizing ourselves in this here book
(I swim into the collective of the group) by
reading about rich people. The book's concern
is advertising. It is an ad for advertising,
& we all are delighted. There is some attempt
in my mind to determine if this be the real rot,

the way men spend their time selling their products.
It is, but is far away

The Cape Elizabeth Town Ladies would bolt in fright
if a real Rice Crispie walked in, or a green giant
so here they are charmed, by someone young enough
to have been their son who has "done well"

The money carries this book. Their interest in
it, the author's interest in it. The author and
they are justly worried about the kids under 25,
who, says the book, are going to "take over" the
world in a few years. *They* don't care about money,
which is why advertising is worried. The ladies
picture them as overrunning hoards (Huns) or Hippies
or messy mongrels, & discuss why they are so "dirty."

It's a very closed room. I become more objective
as the hour wears on, everyone knitting, those who
are not knitting with their eyes straight ahead on
the reader. No one has read the book, except the one
reading from it. They want to be read to, like the
children on the other side of the door who are read
to by Jaycee Wives.

My eyes continually meet those of
        a kindly grandmother who smiles at me.
        She is putting
                    KINDNESS
                                out for me in
her smile like birdseed & I'm too much of a young
proud bigot to smile back.
I defect her glance
& think about how I look, properly dressed,

representing what they are suspicious of,
but camouflaged in their colors, not mine.

The ad man's words come out of the woman's mouth
as she reads. Words like *bread* for money, & we are
again slurping at the world of our children, the
swinging world he represents that we aren't in, being
too much in the box of our detergent. His language
cheapens everything. Death/war made cheaper.

War. Death. Vietnam. War. Death. Vietnam. Killing.
There are bombs being dropped on peasants
mothers nursing/ peasants plowing/ peasants making
lunch
as we sit here reading, being titillated by the advertising
world. Our country is discussing advertising
& its glamorous overworked world at this meeting of
bored Cape Elizabeth matrons while bombing
Haiphong Harbor.

WE ARE RESPONSIBLE.

*   *   *

The ladies don't want to take responsibility.
They don't care about the war; if they do, they're all for it.
(Whatever their husbands want, they want too.)
They don't want to take the responsibility it takes
to read the fucking books every other week.
They want to be read to,
catered to,
protected by the government from Communists,
reassured they will get their Ban-lon
reassured it will be all right.

The country is too big
for them to have very much influence, too big
to understand. The complexity of the vastness
of systems daunts them, much as the workings of
nature & the rise of the stock market
is beyond them. They've given up,
and needing to be entertained, don't want to hear
about others somewhere else dying.

As when I straighten up quickly after stooping, I see
purple on each plot of ground.
There might have been a chance here to live deeply, but
they've lost it, buried in their smug entitlement
& pettiness.

Morning Song

I think you reach a point where you say
well, the window is open a little if I opened
it more I could get more air
& that is how it is with having children,
you can only do so much at one time,
you figure it's going to take twenty years
of your attention & by then you'll be forty-seven,
that's almost fifty and most of my life is over
then, so perhaps it is best to have a choice
& to just say well, I knew quite a bit of what
that world was like & I did not know quite
a bit of what the rest of the world was like,
& it seemed so easy to learn, & in truth
more interesting and as though I did have
the means to learn, that is had writing as a
way to travel lightly & when I wanted, very
heavily, getting quite deeply involved in things
& people, so I just said one Saturday the 11th of
December in 1971 after we had one who was two
and a half, that is Robin was just coming into
the month when his winter equinox would assert
itself, we just said perhaps it won't be so bad
for him alone, not always having another to refer
himself to, mirror himself in & although he will
lack a certain cozy companionship especially when
he goes to bed (remembering that American image
of the two children speaking softly to one another over
their soft dark covers) perhaps our world could
be really alive & constantly changing, not for
a minute getting trapped in housewifery and
limited family squabbles & this is what I thought

& was thinking about as I went about cleaning
up the diapers the toys the dishes in the kitchen
sink that December day when most of the population
was worrying about Christmas shopping & far away
Tibetan yogis were meditating about how to turn
spermic energy back into their metaphysical systems

The Process of Accretion

Poems build.
They have a life
because they're not trying to say anything
they're trying only to discover their own life.

They don't try to speak
in any language but their own
They don't try to be declarative
or facile about anything.

Poems are like clean rugs
and books about designs and patterns
Once you have felt a poem in you
    you're cleaner than you were before.

Like a lot of artistry,
poems work best with a side-winder
kind of focus, more akin to
prayer than comprehensiveness.

The Hawkers

Shadows go by
Hawking visions.
They can't help it,
They've a product to sell,
A meeting-lane to keep.

They duck in & out
Of quick doorways.
They keep a fast-talking staccato
time, as though sight
were fervent & limitless & the change
bouncing in their pockets
could buy a real drink,
a real warmth made of wood
and flame, but I know in gingham & velvet
shadows are only the damned, asleep.
Virgins are the buyers of visions without orgasm
and terrestrial saints are burned
after they have slept with angels.

A Sunday Song

Out of the daily
Out of the sacred day
Out of the rain blessing the day's fall
Out of the lilacs
bending to brush your lips with sweet
    water-drops,
Out of the highway from where we came
       to here,
Out of the book we have learned the Law
Out of our time we learned to use
    what was at hand & in us
Out of our cosmology we perceived
    the dance between us and its rhythms
Out of your mind I seem spun
wake surprised at my separate existence.

The Lesson

I have freed myself from a destructive vision—
Each day
watch my core grow into its own turnings,
even as my fingers find the right chords
finally to play, I exult so much in the lesson
I lose my place and can't read the next note,

and play because exactly this exultation of
performance I haven't felt
in the work of the life,
but as though I were turning myself
inside out like a worn mitten, taking out balls of fuzz
to fit a larger hand in,
so do I sense myself
cutting out suckers which sap my energy
don't use it well,

excursions of thought
and fantasies based on others
a view of others which is media-
based, an endless publicity stunt—

One lifts the pedal when the note is played,
then depresses it, catches it again.
The counting now is not such an obsession,
the notes can be read, but with difficulty.
A tonic is the first note,
a dominant the fifth,
a sub-dominant the fourth.
It comes clear, like paste
well-mixed.

The Second Love Note

*A certain occupational type, living under
certain conditions, upon a certain sum of
money, achieves a certain result in health.*
  —Lura Beam, A *Maine Hamlet*

The apple blossoms I brought inside
to force
are blooming now, Rich

These crabbed branches
tossed, then ripped off by the wind
in that rigid storm that tattered our
heads, to be iced the next day,
are blooming in a coffee can
I covered with blue burlap,
covered the bare table with a green tablecloth,
put them with spring drawings
    & a shell ashtray
beneath the mandala you made of the City
at night, our first and last lettered names
between a baseball and an arrow

I know spring, desire, hope
       gratitude, clarity
when I see it.
Through a long winter
we got,
and now it is so simple: fucking you
makes my headache go away.

Altruism

No one told me it was the fashion around here to go to the midnight church service so Robby and I drove in at 10 o'clock Christmas morning and went to church. For him it was the first time. We were lucky. There were hardly any people and no choir, just the organist and a few ministers and a few hardy single people but no other children. We sang hymns, I took communion, and Rob listened intently and didn't squirm much at all, but was happy when it was over. The minister quoted C.S. Lewis and Charles Williams which I thought amazing and asked why we didn't have courage to love other people given that Christ had so *much* courage. He wanted to know why it wasn't more obvious when Christ was born, given that God could have made it so. And why didn't God save Christ from his horrible death, given that he certainly could have?

"I want to know why! " he said, as though it were the question he had been carrying around with him all week, in much the same way I would have phrased my main question: I want to know why my body is cut off from feeling, and how I have gotten year by year more deeply into a dangerous physical-psychological situation. The minister answered that God probably did it all like this to make us work for the answer. He indicated that the same courage it takes us to take a chance on people and be hurt was the same courage it took Christ to do his deeds, even the deed of being born, without being bailed out. He thought "being bailed out" from life was not a good idea, that we should realize we're stuck here and chin up, make the best of it. There were a lot of hidden messages here, a warmed-over Calvinism which reminded me of my mother's Methodist church she'd rejected for our Episcopal parish, involved now in resettling Hmong refugees.

The uneasy dualism and paternalism of Christianity which has had me come last of all to myself as an object of interest or focus, after family, husband, children, was working right along in everything said in this church service: to love yourself you must love others first.

Whew.

I think that's not right. I don't believe it anymore. I think it takes more courage to take a chance on one's self/go for broke on your own steam and become responsible for your own garbage—carefully, without hypocrisy, than to selflessly help other people. My step-grandmother was a Grey Lady, helping others in hospitals all her life, but she barely talked to us, the grandchildren who came with her second marriage. Now she's in a home for people who can't remember a thing. What happens to people when they literally lose their minds, while their bodies are just fine? The details of people suddenly escape?

Here is a detail about you.

Here is another detail about you, and you.

But if they are not anchored to the core of myself, that core formless and changing, day by day, year by year growing into a complex molecular model, I will forget everything. Or it's unpreventable.

When you have a family, and so many of your actions are for other people, taking time for yourself feels like chipping out from a glacier. But it may be the central issue of being thirty-two, for me.

The Score and the Accompaniment

> *Learning to beat the source of relation.*
> —Edward Dorn, *The Garden of Birth*

MOMMY MOMMY COME DOWN HERE
What is it Robin?
I need you to get another graham cracker
        yellow raisins for me.
You've had enough now.
What?
Me?
Enough?

Mindless bumping of feet on the high chair.
One reaches adulthood to spend all their
time with children and the minds of children.

Children are left out of liberation talk
not because they aren't there but because they
must be subtracted to start with the premise
of an adult: a functioning human being (if the
damage hasn't been too severely done, if the
mind is not completely retarded or frozen in
fear, having hidden behind the skirts of children
as behind, earlier, the skirts of the mother)

able to decide what to do with a life. If you
add children, immediately the argument becomes
subverted and dominated: as in real life the
child can dominate over the functioning mind,
in an argument the needs and desires of children

are so insistent (the future of the species!)
that they immediately become the *excuse* for the
retardation of adult happiness. A woman dominated
by children is an entirely different species
from a functioning adult. She is mad.

& yet
had I not this child here
who is playing now quietly safely & happily
would I even be home
would I have such an excuse
          to be here in the house
          writing on an April afternoon
could I create the remarkable tensions
out of another life—
Could I see yellow for yellow,
watch how language is learned by the human,
see what structures strike visually
& what is ignored,
catch what companionship is
                    among one's own age-group
                    & older ones & younger ones
flash on the remarkable perceptions
I did not teach
but which are being learned.

Learner, you are teaching me so much.

Tensors

I walk up the path to the dorm, filming. I am taking shots of my life, of my self as a representative woman, and doing a continuous shooting everywhere I go, retrospectively looking at my life, sometimes in satire, sometimes with bitter irony that it should have ended up this way, such a shambles of a life, sometimes with rich deep fulfillment that I have been so lucky. So rare! To have such a life, to have such opportunities that I can do just what I want, and only have to identify that.

The November air is sunny, crisp. The grasses are a deep green, no brown yet, it has not yet been so cold that the grasses have devolved into their protective brown.

I am too free, and it settles into a kind of loneliness, a use of solitude that I am only beginning to savor. The deep browns. The deep purple vistas of being alone. I think to cast myself onto a rock, like a piece of lichen—and move away when something is no longer comfortable. Just now I practiced, actually up for doing it but after a while my attention wandered, I could take in no more and needed to feel a deeper connection to something, to someone, or to myself. I picture my book: the shape, the parts it is made up of, the salvaging job. I picture who I will write a letter to—and picture the recipients, see them also wandering in a kind of haze, not much different than mine except perhaps more embroiled in a role from a job, reacting to, relating to that, instead of a work.

The long definitions of a work: how the connotations change each day; how each day begins again an attempt to carry on what one is doing, to improve it, to shape it, to get it out in a form that is readable to others. To catch the Beautiful Thing! Sometimes I do it, and the work is pervasive as an orgasm, seems to be speaking in a voice fuller than my own being, to express the mystery that it did come out of me, but from where?

And that is why others around me explore very far back, to pre-Greek human endeavor, because they sense that it is not just now that makes up one's voice. It is also the voice of the Phoenician fisherman, of Enkidu losing his tie to Gilgamesh, as that power-hungry king abandons friendship for dominion and loses humanity.

Absence

Sleep would nestle around my head,
it would be all right
except visions of icy paddles
hitting my head repeatedly
crawl into bed with me

No one
to cuddle with, to bend my form round
to give the underlying additional heat
and my own warmth isn't enough—

So I am freezing. My chest begins to hollow out
No fire downstairs because I didn't make one
and you aren't here,
I have to make the house warm myself.

I get up to put knee socks on and 2 shirts and a sweater,
the night stretches with all its holes,
too thin, too long bone-brittle cold

Suddenly my smallest action is a worry. Peace I had woven,
albeit determinedly
from coffee & scrapbook & music & dancing children
has splintered into this jagged edge
once they sleep.
I wait for the cut into morning.

Do you know what a relief daylight is
sunlight in the grey dawn
to the sleeper huddled, buried
under blankets, still shivering?

Death of the Animus

I'm living with another woman in a small town like Plainfield. I don't know any inhabitants but they know me. A man comes to the door, threatening me. I pick him up easily and tip him upside down, knock his head again and again against the steep stairs outside. Finally he's dead and can't hurt me anymore. I hadn't meant to kill him but at least it'll stop him from impinging on me.

I wander around the village with him in my arms, a crushed flat body. I can't figure out what to do with him—whether I'm "guilty of murder" so should try to "dispose of the body" or whether none of this applies to me and I'm free of these rules too. Maybe I can just go to the police—it seems that's what people used to do when encountering death on one's hands. They are on my path around the village square, so I toddle in.

(A couple is rehearsing ballet adagio in a house for sale across the street. Very attractive to me so I stop and watch for a minute). The police say he was already dead almost from taking too many cough drops, not to worry. They are nice, rather distracted, not very interested in my case but well-meaning. It's not a big deal to them. They're playing with their CB radios.

The character I killed was tall and dressed in a black suit, thin, young-looking and drab. Not spirited—he didn't put up a fight. He's so out of it there's no good reason why he should want to live.

I wake thinking this is lust being killed matter-of-factly for spiritual gain. I feel somewhat relieved that all this didn't happen, but as I write this I know also that it did.

Tooth, Hand, and Nail

She fought her husband. She thought he was to blame for everything. If she was able to pin it on him, then she wouldn't have herself to blame, and she could still be a North American Martyr. It was so peaceful being a martyr. They had wings, they committed suicide, they cried while others were uncomfortable in their dry eyes, they thought it would all end.

But it didn't. The next morning after throwing her horror scene she got up and looked in the mirror and was shocked to see her eyes were terribly swollen, simply from crying. No one had hit her. No one had told her what to read or where to go or where not to go. No one had kicked her out in the world, taken away her money, stolen her children, or deserted her. She had no one to blame but herself for her swollen eyes. She began blaming the footstool, which she must have run into the night before in the dark.

Out of Practice

She knew she had to go practice because if she didn't, she wouldn't be getting anything out of it. She had to have discipline. That's what makes the world go around. People in the dorm were smoking dope, and she could think of others who were hassled by their children now, and she wasn't, so really, she should use this spare time and go practice.

When she got to the piano she stared at it and it seemed to rise up on itself and bite her hand. It was a good excuse. Pianists always were hurting their hands and then they were not able to practice for a while. She would tell her teacher the next day that the piano had bitten her hand and that's why she couldn't practice. But she was out of practice at lying so she supposed she would simply be embarrassed again at not having learned the notes better.

One More Time

She kept inviting him over. She had to import his body into her living room always just one more time, to get a last glimpse. She kept wanting to have dinner with him, and so they did, but he was a curious mixture of passivity and aggression. She was beginning to understand that two things were possible: one, either he spent all his aggression on the college, where he fought campaigns with many soldiers using the most brutal and intricate of weaponry and had no aggression left for his personal life, or,

two, he didn't like her and never thought to call *her*.

What she wanted was to be called, adored, summoned. She wanted to be Helen to her Achilles, Cassandra to her Agamemnon. She thought of herself as the mysterious sign bearer, who knows things without having to be told, who walks around on the ramparts, watching the battle from above and dropping signs, signals, which only those most enlightened, like her Achilles, could see. The difference was that he really *was* fighting, whereas she was really not walking around on the ramparts, but home mending the children's things, where she should have been, or up at Northwood practicing the piano. He thought he was fighting for his life, because the college and his self had become One in a non-mystical transformation.

He was more existentialist than alchemist. When she was cocky and lively he took it as being too strong, brittle, especially bitchy. She had a whole life going, which filed quietly out the door whenever he appeared, so involved was she in him. And, in truth, she had always been this way, had erased any trace of her personality when men were around. But she was attracted, wasn't she, so wasn't that worth it? What she dreaded was getting in a fight with him. She dreamed of mysterious .38s and .45s showing up in hidden places, that one day he would shoot her absolutely dead. It would be worth dying for—but what exactly was it?

Human Form in Prison

Here is a love note to
a world where madness and sanity sit
back to back on the shelf

of another's expectations of order.
I come in and the other
is always worried

about what I might do.
It's as though I have a crysknife
tucked into my shirt,

that I am too capable of hurt,
that I must blunt myself
because I am too strong,

too sharply piercing.
The other must be quite afraid.
The fact that my child

talks constantly of poisons now
probably isn't irrelevant.
Perhaps we are poisoning

one another, in trying to produce
domestic harmony.
If pleasure is a word we are too old for,

and meaning is only to be found in books,
that leaves me
with a knife in my belt,

waiting for a hole in the net
I might enlarge
to escape.

Everyone who comes
I pounce on as allies
in my attempt.

At the prison the guards are so lax
prisoners pile picnic tables
& climb over the walls.

The officials laugh nervously
and say there's no drug problem
in the institutions.

What do they talk about in their meetings?
They talk about poisoning one another,
but they talk in political terms

and mainly try to keep out
divisive elements.

Once you are a threat to one
penal institution
you are a threat
to them all.

The Choreographer

When you set a dance on a person that is magical
no other dancer can ever come along and dance it exactly
because all the movements, the curve of the arms and
fall of the weight were worked out with your first joy
at the choreography trying to grasp onto that original dancer's
body which fits it like a new glove

And though someone
can travel from London to Stockholm to Stuttgart setting
Mr. B's dances on this and that company,
no one can ever dance it like
Farrell or Kent or Kirkland,
the memory of those created roles
is like the original bronze casting, indelible in the early
critic's memory who saw the part first with the original dancer

And is that not how the life goes
after-images trooping behind us of the few stellar experiences
we must have been created for. They are really enough.
At the young age of thirty-two I think I've lived enough
of the really great ones to be only making further
permutations of actual occasions, draping them onto everyone
whether each fits very well or not

So walking around in my life are shambles of ghosts, who
drape themselves rather baggily in their costumes,
the best are the ones which seem to fit, and the ones who go all
the way home with me glimmer like the original,
like a doll up in the attic I never brought down.

Leaving California

1.

when I get home
I want to cover all the pillows
with rich deep spider-cloth
and find all my lost kittens
tame them again

Conduct most meetings by candlelight
so our living room won't have such access
to the commonplace

I want to store up in my lungs
that good deep full rich air of Vermont
and watch the river carefully
and ride my bike over to your house
and teach you shiatsu
or maybe just do it on you
so you can see how unafraid of touching
I have become

2.

It'll be interesting being in Vermont again
like "Look, Ma, I'm flying!
See? I can live here too!"
Look Ma, I can adapt anywhere,
I can live anywhere, in anyplace,
upon any planet, in any slime,
in anyone's boot, on anyone's island, on
anyone's lobsterback, "Look Ma, here I am again!"

It'll be that freaking quiet.
I'm afraid of the moisture that'll
    get underneath my vertebrae
And no crazy people
And it so green, so sane
Nobody watching the hummingbirds
And what will I do in that calm
in that bleakness   how will I run from
    my kitchen when it begins rolling me up
in its linoleum floor?

3.

This is how it goes in my world

Wendell tells people about lobster-fishing
in the Oceanarium in Bar Harbor
because there aren't enough lobsters to fish.
But the thing doesn't flow right
and the man won't change the exhibit

Diane covers her notebooks with the most lovely
collages   they become precious magical lapis
she will put the postcards of various angels on them
she has just brought from Italy

Her rooms are like her notebooks
all the spaces are sacred
Her life becomes like that too, guarded
She controls it, utterly in a way few of us do

Paul comes down from Idaho to Berkeley
he speaks very quietly

I think how terrified all my family in Denver will be
when I am hardly speaking at all
Silence can be the ultimate weapon
What you do say suddenly becomes very important
when you say very little
And you have time to watch.
Spiders speak hardly at all
just build their complicated webs everywhere
When too big a catch gets in and pulls the whole
thing down, they let the intruder lumber away,
Then lug the strands back up to the starting point
and start all over.

Whenever the people in my world seem to shine
with a certain brilliance
my world seems OK again

4.

What I miss after my father's
death is
his connection to the dissolute

I have the fantasy he would
like my work and dig it for himself,
not place it at arm's length to not be
discussed if one can help it
as the rest of my family does

it seems to create some awkwardness

My mother is mainly happy
when we discuss her love life

the old boyfriend now in his 80s in Florida
so I do that as much as possible

but underneath my feet is seeping a
cold dark black sewer
I try to bang the head of the intruder
hard again and again
against the stone steps

and then I carry his body around in my
arms throughout the whole village,
asking,
what should I do with it?

5.

I don't feel my father's presence.
I feel his absence. He's under the ground
and in tribute to his lack of spiritual
consciousness, I think of him atomized
into zillions of tiny particles.

Fragment

She didn't particularly trust him, and she *really* didn't trust herself with him. She had, as usual, known him too well in fantasy. They had experienced too much, in dreams, in the early morning waking hours when she pulled him up around her neck like a warm blanket, warding off the day. In life, she had no idea what he would do or what was proper or what he was thinking of when he looked blank at her, seeming to stare. Maybe he was blank. Looks which she took two weeks ago to mean some special connection to her, she realized now could just be a rather blank countenance on the world.

Her ideal was to be able to gather up the fullness of one's being and bring to another person all the richness one has seen in life, like a gift. She thought her body probably showed exactly what she had been through in her life, and even the act of talking with someone was an intimate thing, if one was really connected to this vehicle of multiple histories. She was approaching a new morality: making love was an ultimate generosity, a chance to tumble out this past non-verbal history like a dance. One would feel richly the pervasive gentleness flowing to all parts of the body, the legs and thighs and arms and groin warming in giving out and taking in all this from another person giving it all too. Such a gift was so sacred, so powerful that it could not be given very many times; the explosions which resulted emotionally from such an exchange were not for a person to know too often. The intensity of being thus with another person was great enough that the rest of the time should be spent alone, in contact with one's self only, if only to process the reverberations from such exchanges and store up reserves.

As she met men who continually had no idea what she was talking about she began to see that they had different moralities. They were interested in conquest, and she was the prey. She began to feel hunted. Soon she took no chances, and didn't stray out alone.

The good clean snow. The patterns of snow in the crisp morning.

The Stranger

I notice that most of the world
is trying to water down
the language one has tried so hard
to uncover

It's the same process, the editors do,
the mothers do, the fathers I make my men into,
they want a little more class
a little more relation to the world at large
a little more plain-speaking

In therapy groups the leaders are especially
suspicious of language
"Too many words," they say
and when I am about to cry,
"I hear tears!"
as though it is a victory: See, we're successful
at undermining your basic confidence!

What kind of radical vultures *are* these
reporters, editors, interviewers, therapists?
These are my friends?
This is an economy I participate in?
These are people who would be my friends
only if I were to be like them,
only if I made myself consciously in their image,
scrawny and unsure and terrified of the world

I would have to be
a spider living underwater,
fueled by a shiny bubble

into which she drags her prey for safekeeping,
forgetting all the variable images of the world
she once knew

Family in the Desert

Look how easily he goes out the door.
He fairly glides, like a knife in water
or a man going through a mirror
to meet his Death.

He goes out the door easily
because I am here.
Mommy and Baby are at home,
where they should be,
stoking the fire, cleaning the floors,
taking care of each other.

Daddy likes to do the going-out.
He doesn't like Mommy to be out
and him home alone;
it's not cozy without Mommy there.
He *really*
doesn't like Mommy driving far,
or at night,
because she might trip
on a sense of herself that is strong
and can explore the world
and her Death
without Daddy.

No Time to Breathe

I've been away quite some time
from the northeast,
but I know when I get back it will seem
like no time—will we all have the grace
to pick up where we left off?

The trains of Berkeley go whistling through
at about 9:30 p.m., the children finally asleep—
quiet moves in, lonely like the fog coming on us,
the brisk rustle of the night sea breeze,
a sax next door beginning to play
windows to shut & lock in this helter-skelter
neighborhood

Listening earlier,
Robby & I talk about trains coming down
from Sacramento, up from L.A.
the California Zephyr from the rest of the country
freight trains by the Bay preparing
to begin again to cross the country,
their mournful whistles and clattering—

Finish your story, I said,
when he couldn't think of any more to be said.
A story should not be left unfinished—
Like our lives: something we're happy with
when its time to go.

The Betrayal of the Body

> *to passionately affirm and reaffirm …*
> —Barbara Hepworth

The form of my father's life
was deviousness.

Since he could express no voice
or no feeling, he ringed himself
with tiny small pleasures
which never grappled with the size
of a man's need.

He went to the PenCol Drug for a sundae.
Maddened, my mother burrowed deep
into martyrdom, losing herself as she slithered.
She would need the best of the world's *richesse* to keep her afloat.
She would need bubbles & buoyancy, some kind of deliberate
love, not a marriage balled as an old sweater.
She would need to *glide.*

This was a woman unclear about her essential aims,
weighted down in a world my dad arranged
without mutuality.
                    She cut out.
When I came along, declaring the world
viable, and possibly mine,
she was maddened into torment.

Far along in a process of encasing her body
in paint, she turned outward & *became* a painter.
She laughed, cracking years of orange terra-cotta

& Plaster of Paris from her thighs, draping her arms
with magenta.
When she began to dance again
we marveled at the power of a body
to sustain life.

The Miner's Daughter

The shape of my father was
caved-in.

His stomach muscles were dead from polio.
The groin shouldn't have had feeling,
but it did. He was alive. Not working with
a full deck, but still *here*.

The shape of his body didn't hold him back.
One leg shorter, he clambered over hillsides
and gold tailings with a Geiger counter.

It's true he didn't breathe from his stomach—
chest hollowed out, neck
a chunk of wood hovering atop a curved bowl.
His arms became strong; he used them to
deliver people into the Western sky.

No one wins in war, he got that.
He realized he'd been spared going,
though he'd *wanted* to.
He piled on experiences with no looking back
what they mean by *he had a lease on life*.
An amazing legacy for me.

Tree base   fish base   rock base
basalt base
Get it rock bottom clear what you come from.
We mine granite around here, not uranium,

We mine one of the hardest substances in the world.
Shined, it can be beautiful, more
than you can say about uranium.
Granite is pretty expensive,
as are all the parts of our bodies.

Hello, Darkness

This is the way the world sounds:
        very quietly.

It moves along—just when you have it
        resolved into a structure,
there it goes again, moving off

My thoughts vibrate as they approach
a higher note,
you can hear me debating
whether to fix a resolve or go on …
        and then dropping it, to let
what happens be born, *to issue the sun.*

The world, really,
is so quiet.
We're the noisy ones, retching
in our demands and judgments,
making ourselves unhappy, stirring up trouble.

We squeeze the night down into tiny orifices
a screen we can't get through.
        The night isn't small.
        It opens vastly, same landscape as
day, only black. Unlike a cat,
we're no good in pure dark
stagger around, fearing large animals.

Unable to sleep,
I throw myself out of bed
to the living room couch   more spacious.

It's the same night downstairs, the same blackness.
The quality is more permeable
     I can move freely through it.

Returning to bed after sitting outside
I turn out the light in Miranda's room,
wonder if she will mind the dark.
She doesn't.
Slow trees, slow air, slow being.
     Let me be calmer, more sure—
Come into new being
this fall

New Poems

Some Inner Darkness Therein

Practicing Ba Gua Pond Circle on Mt. Desert

We walk around the pond
at The Whole Health Center,
eaves slant like canyon rock shale

Looking at a small pedestal
in the center of the circle
the purple glass orb is adversity.
We want to keep our eye on this
Dark Magic, work to transform it.

Inside arm stretches high,
palm facing out
Lower hand limns the rim of the circle
palm open
The orb has changed to a skittery Other
who we watch with calm focus

Evil, or some one who wishes
you harm. Mean girls grown up.
Psychopaths projecting on someone
outside themselves. Or
the part of yourself which equivocates,
gives up, drifts into depression.

The movement is an ocean of beauty—
just doing it fills you with hope and excitement.

235

Paul shows how to draw your foot along,
flat, not heel then toe, like
people usually walk.

The lyricism masks a powerful kinetic
energy. Do this right, & it could help you
repel danger, even from yourself,
those moments when you're hurting
yourself without knowing it.

Ribs expand, mind clicks into alert;
Stalactites of ice
light your eyes with courage.

Ba Gua is peering into
the abyss of challenges, Beloved,
drawing breath up sharply
through the nose, expelling spent *chi*
through the mouth.

It's thrilling. My heart
surges with love for this work,
Paul teaching it, the *value* of having it here.

Makes me want to live on Mt. Desert
for the next twenty years,
get old with these people and
help them die,
Let them help me live,
and then die.

Gloucester, Various Histories

That which frees you from your tiny self is love.
—Khaqani Shirwani

Catch everything, Beloved.

Catch the chickadee discovering no food
    at the feeder
Catch my excitement
    walking around Gloucester with Gerrit,
his town, Olson and Ferrini's town

Olson concerned to see Gloucester a well run *polis*
as Maximus to Gloucester
a citizen involved with where he lived,
publicly, artistically, historically
showing up at town council meetings

Gloucester, with its multiple histories,
and heroes.
I embrace the layers, feel the richness
of early Dogtown through Olson,
Gerrit, Ferrini, and now Charles Peter and Ferrini's
son's film & Peter Anastas' history

We look out from Fort Square, a
sweet small park now, Richard does t'ai chi
we stare out over the shore holding on to
a smart brass railing   There's a play structure
for kids   We look at the plaque
commemorating that Charles lived upstairs

Seeing Gloucester with Gerrit:
so precious, Beloved—but the missing years!
I torture myself about the decades which tumbled
when I *didn't* get to know Gerrit
Where *was* I?

Time works as it does for a reason

Across from his house, Stage Fort Park
on Hough Avenue—
my name. My dad and grandfather, from Red Lodge,
Montana, were Governors of the Colorado
Mayflower Society, their ancestor, William Brewster

The first permanent settlement of the
Massachusetts Bay Colony was in 1623:
     men anchored their ships in the harbor,
     set up fish stages—drying platforms
on Fishermen's Field

Miles Standish and Capt. Wm. Pierce
     tried to take over the stages in 1625
fought, settling their fight at this huge rock

Looking out
you can imagine the fish houses on wharves,
the drying racks from Annisquam to Pigeon Point

Peter Anastas shows that Charles' concern
to preserve specific houses &
parts of Gloucester in urban renewal
was heard by Paul Kenyon, editor of the *Gloucester
Daily Times*   He reached an audience of
12,000 readers in editorials & poems he

sent to the newspaper, talked often before
city council as a citizen. He would have liked these
National Heritage Sites all over town,
"building, growing, sustaining our sense of place"
He was responsible for influencing an earlier generation
of town fathers and city planners to
value Gloucester's history from 1965 on

We leave Gloucester, drive back up to Mt. Desert
I resolve to be around Gerrit more,
listen to him play the piano & talk
while there's time

We're Not Going Home Yet

Finding sleep, finding somewhere to go
          to be comfortable,
          a self one can live with
which meets in the dark
          that person you really are—

The birds are voracious
eat
everything put in the feeders right away,
We don't even know if it's different birds
or the same few

We're leaving for Berkeley
ten days later than last year

I should be able to manage this
but the darkness of the woods
rises up,
Plummeting temperatures throw me
I buy big warm felt slippers
At Walmart, haunt the thrift store
buy sweaters, warm boots
the troops come out
to deal with acute loneliness

Thrown back on one's
own resources
I reach down to the lake,
The moon is hovering there,
          beginning to rise high
          big full round yellow

Look around
There's much to support
the stranger in the wilderness

Stop the internal chiding
comparing yourself to others
The small black chickadee
doesn't think about his Self.

Authentic Movement

Developed in the 1970s by dancers creating non-performance forms of movement. No movement not prompted from within.

My heart is heavier this summer
without Karel,
who started this Mt. Desert group—
she died, quickly and suddenly this winter

People grieved together here all winter and spring,
their grief drifting among snow, ice, wind,
new spring   I'm way behind,
still trailing it as we begin

It comes back to me, this work;
the body seeks wildness,
freedom, solace, individuation.
No marching orders from outside
no sound but your own.
Movement from within.

Julie's inert,
arms slung across a bolster.
She may never move—a crocodile log.
Later, what's that banging on the floor?
I turn to look—hey, it's her. What gumption!
Of course: the possibilities of *sound*.

My feet hanker to zig and zag the air in
Egyptian hieroglyphics,

body facing front/head and feet sideways.
You can want to *not* move.
Many do nothing for a long time.
Elastic time, warpy silence are music
Weslea plays with ropes, not stretching.
Patricia entangles arms and feet in a
Gordian knot, hard to unloose.

Limits are what we're inside of, Olson said.
It's a relief to pare down
when you're drowning in overwhelm.

Out the tall window, Patricia's *rosa rugosa*
tall and bushy in mid-August.

The studio dims with dusk;
out the windows,
black.

We hold warmth for a while in a large circle
marvelously enclosing,
then diffuse in the night.
Separate fireflies, loosed
to island roads.

Maine Songs

The door
drifts open. Cat?
Ah, we left them at home.
Breeze.

Sadness,
to not have them here.
You can't have everything, my parents
used to say
trying to impress limits on my exploratory
style

Why not? I thought.
Why not try for it all?

I have, and have seen
why limits are a good idea

Overwhelmed
    we squabble and joust
    stabbing the smallest things

Aware of reactivity,
    we seem incapable
of stopping it.

Picture rolling your anger up in a garland of roses
throwing it out to space,
then blowing it up

That's what Berkeley Psychic Institute recommends
It *would* slow you down, I say, considering
trying to picture how shifting gears
    enough to do this silly joyful act
might impede angry words
rolling from my mouth like cartwheels

Eight Weeks

Don't you think you've gotten more manly, Raul, more
masculine, since fatherhood? My sister-in-law says this
dreamily to her husband, watching
her exuberant child surrounded by family

A few heads snap up this late afternoon Christmas day
another round of presents from aunts cousins friends grandparents
who all look on, audience for the antics of this beloved girl-child
who growls when addressed.

She's looking for more packages with a big E for Emily,
has recovered from anguish over the towering marble run
toppled a moment ago by an errant foot.
Vectors of family closeness keep us intimate; we look on quietly
but with love as my grandparents used to, not saying much.
I think I can see love brimming around the room in waves.

An uncle is engaged in the Seven Planes of Consciousness.
Adi the highest plane, Monadic the higher octave of the intellect—
what we're enacting here by the tree
is a low sub-level of the Physical,
where we frolic with hope and good will

The Emotional Etheric is where first experiments
with the astral body will land you ...
But let's return to that tree: not huge, like "The Nutcracker" tree
which suddenly shoots up after the parturient curtain rises;
still, it's nicely full, to 4 yr. old Emily, it may tower.

She sits next to it looking up at the hanging ornaments,
a few spinning.

Sisters-in-law are unreliable narrators, especially when daydreaming
about pregnancy. Marga watches her brother's wife appraise a gift
of a loamy green shirt, the color the tree would be
left in the forest.
She thinks about her own breasts

plumping up. She has heard that milk letting down
reverberates like a harp deep in the pudenda,
twangs like a stringed instrument.
She would like this pendulousness when the ducts swell,
the harp throbbing deep inside her.
All curtain-opener for the Astral Plane
where droplets of *prana* dance.

This newly achieved second pregnancy subtext
too fragile to mention publicly.
Wasn't it touching she said that to Raul? Loving, really,
Marga says to her husband as they drive home,
envying her sister-in-law's insouciant naturalness, wanting for
herself an obstreperous child, the fragile second pregnancy.

Beasts

The animals
are outside
they don't want
to be inside

with us; they're
wild, after all

wouldn't know what
to do with
themselves, would
pace and come
up against the walls
as they do
in zoos
or as we do
when we want out

They aren't *domesticated*
We can't hug them

they don't
want to be hugged.
They would like
to *eat* us.

Or turn and
amble away, like the large
brown mother bear
lumbering back into
the night from the

clearing,
like the feral cat
taking off
after slurping

milk I put out
for it.

The Clairvoyant

What did we want
from his talk?
Not talk really,
but that he
should be transcendent,
give us a taste of his power.
That's all we cared about.

If he could do this thing,
see into our minds,
teleport, read our auras,
tell if they were discolored
or tarnished, drooping like
angel's wings, lost
their round shape
pulled into a spheroid,
lagging, us somehow *ahead*
of our aura and it
rushing to catch up,
were we about to
step on it? & what then?

We wanted a taste of how it works,
where his sight came from.
Okay, a demonstration.
Or not, if it was secret.
But *about that*. Nothing else.

We didn't care about his politics
how many children he had;
his close relationship with a

Hopi leader from Hotevilla,
or the Dalai Lama—along about
then it occurred to us he was
name-dropping. Our
minds somersaulted
the Reiki Master
began doing yoga
in the back.

We took any mention of the
profane or secular as cardboard filler,
it gave us a headache
made us want to walk around
to listen to this
rambling. We weren't being valued;
the time we were taking to
put our behinds on these chairs,
nothing to him.

His eyes rolling upwards?
Not a hit from the divine,
but him thinking where
to ramble to next.

That's just it.
If he'd talked for even
a nanosecond about being an agent of
a superior force,
how his body feels
when this energy from on high
slams through him
we'd have pricked up our ears—
tell us about that! we would have
all breathed in unison

But he just liked to hear himself talk,
far past exhaustion

The words kept plopping down—
maddening, their
lack of value to him
with increasing self-importance &
self-anointed authority

Outside, clear notes of
a warbler!
Energy, stamina, among the daffodils.

Two Fences

Palestine

They dart down like quick rats
from their beds
in the packing crates
to their jobs building high rises
in the Israeli part of Gaza

Working construction was
never so dangerous,
dodging Israeli security forces
who will arrest &
imprison them
for trying to get to work.
Hades, or *No Exit*, Purgatorio,
their homeland too!
A wall cutting them off from
their livelihood

Mexico

Insanity, again
don't we know how sick
walls are
haven't we been through
Berlin and the DMZ
between South and North Vietnam?
The Great Wall of China?
When has a wall not been
among the harshest,

least humanitarian of solutions
mankind can devise

In Nogurra the wilderness animals
are screaming
their feeding grounds
on the other side of a
20 ft. cement wall

The Tree of Rand

Berkeley lectures of Yvonne Rand, June 2010

This is how she spoke:
plain narrative.
Talk-stories from a woman
simple on the outside, corn-silks
complicated inside. Long skirt,
black first-grade-straight hair,
gimpy knees, sitting on the chair
feet apart, in meditation
hands forming a small chapel.

Pay attention to the changes
that are not a thrill, she sd.
They will be daunting, they will catch you up
in the throat like a bad novel,
or a good novel dipped into thriller.
The expectations give us trouble are
those that surprise us. Observe, identify,
describe them. Which do you dread
more, your own or your partner's dying?

*

Poppies scatter so many seeds!
Do the same. Let your work touch many.
If a child dies before a parent, we say it's tragic,
not the natural order. But many seeds
die, not all take root. In a litter of fifteen brown bears,
not all the cubs will make it.

*

The opposite of judgment is acceptance.

*

It's important to have a witness to your process
so you're not talking to the walls.

The more specific you can be, the better.
Note change. Don't get caught up in story.

*

When you sit at a table of gossips,
keep quiet. Be the person who doesn't
join in. Eventually people will hear
the cattiness of what they're saying.

*

Listen to what's up for another
without reactivity, judgment
or even comment. When listening—
really listen, do only that.
That's useful, and supportive—loving.

*

The Mark of Change is Impermanence—
a change we don't relish.

She asks us to think about Regret.

What do you regret?
What you didn't do, but stay caught in.
Let it go.

Transformation happened then anyway,
keeps happening as you tell the old story
again and again. Realize you can change it—
nothing stays the same. Vary your tellings,
an upbeat ending this time, a bird's eye view
next time as you understand with more perspective.
Try to find what might have actually
happened rather than only your own angst
or crisis—not the Ancient Mariner's tale of woe
which you carry like a worn blankey.
Let it go. Let it float to tangle with stars
and planets—how much lighter you'll be!

*

As you get older, there are new things to regret.
We didn't ask our parents
about their lives when they were younger
rather than too old, regret that we
pushed them away, didn't
embrace them with compassion. Now they're gone.
Too late for them or us to enjoy one another.

*

So the question is: how do I contribute to the permanence
of this situation? Sometimes you want to build a
different thing than you've got.
So how do I habitually reinforce this one so
it hangs around?
It's o-o-over, sings Roy Orbison
Keep a journal of permanence/impermanence—
Note when you're dragging embers
of the old order in your tail-feathers
making it hard for the new ones to get established.

Underneath aversion is fear.
You may turn away or turn towards,
but underneath is still fear.

Figure out what you're afraid of
or if someone's afraid of you, get clear why

Once Yvonne had emptied
the trash at the Zen Center—
she emerged from behind the building
to a huge lug on the street
pointing a knife at her.

DON'T YOU DARE! she yelled.
Her voice boomed, a force itself,
not a cry for help, but the thunder of outrage
that he could blaspheme humanity by thinking
to harm *her — or anyone!*

She lunged with both arms pointed sharp
at the attacker's face. *He's the same height as my son,*
she was thinking   Forceful maternal outrage at
no respect for *whoever*
she was, a human being
wise woman shaman, revered Senior Teacher
at the Zen Center—
The guy ran away.

*

Don't get involved in storytelling.
Don't stir the pot; let the muck soften and settle.

*

Why does one procrastinate?
Fear. The task is awesome.
Break it down, small bites each day.
Soon you will *want* to work on it,
be looking forward to the next morning. Know
what you will do, plan it the night before.
If you're stuck,
Make a date with yourself. A quota of pages:
20 pages, five poems a day.
Keep your date as seriously as you would
meeting someone for coffee.

*

Don't mind another's mind.
You can only change you.
Stay present to yourself. Don't get muddled,
lost in others' imperatives.

Beware a person who only asks questions.
They want to keep you away.
People who can't look you in the eye
are afraid. They may intend harm
don't trust them. Never let your guard down.

*

Beware one who sets him or herself up
as perfect, then lectures to the world, judge
and jury. You're so outside, a heathen not
even fit to be at the table.

*

Yvonne tells us what she didn't see,
didn't understand. She's not afraid to
reveal a mind in process. Isn't anyone you really
love like that? It's called modesty, humility.

*

Love is not compliance or obligation.
Love is not standing in judgment of others.
Love is enjoying spontaneity,
feeling loose and easy with one another.
Sometimes to know what you lack
you have to understand where you don't have it,
you have to review what love *is*.

Love is easy laughter with another,
confidence and enjoyment in
contributing to building trust.
A person who destroys trust to feel good
may not be capable of love. A person who demands
false sentimentality and can't tell it from
authentic positive feeling is—sad.

We are not scared feral cats who must run.
We are sacred tame cats who choose to stay.
Royal, elegant in our love, beloved.
> *The true measure of our practice*
> *is how much we can open to others.*

Be an open camera shutter.
Love watches others stumble, &
encourages them gently to begin again,
admits her own stumbles, moving on
together, to do better. Love is not a grown up
mean girl keeping score.

Love is kind; not jealous or competitive.
You *ward-off* an enemy.
Love is not affect or mask: *what you see should be what you get.*

Develop a capacity for presence.
You won't be able to stand your ground
if you're involved in attraction and aversion.

*

In Kauai Nonilanders let the rain fall on them
in the quick downpours, let their
skin be nourished, a form of staying open,
looking for the positive in every negative.

*

The Heart Sutra: everything changes.
Nothing remains the same. A succession
of waves—each one different but connected.
Your task is to wait and
ride them in.

Be around large animals—horses, cattle, bears,
elephants—they repay in trust,
communicate in broad moves
milking, the tail of the cow flings around—
whap! in the face.

*

Beware people who use small children
as pawns, mirrors, or extensions of themselves.
They move people around on a checkerboard,
slot in whoever serves the current need.
Hell to pay if you don't stay in your tiny assigned role.

261

The child raised by this Queen of Hearts
catches on fast, soon as a sense of self develops—
she doesn't love me for myself. I'm a play toy to amuse her.
Walking on eggshells, dreading (like everyone else) when
one will overstep the narrow precipice she demands:
next it'll be me. The Queen of Hearts is a scared little girl,
still bellowing *"Off with his head!"*

Retirement I

> *Men marry what they need.*
> *I marry you.*
>   —my godfather, John Ciardi

What I wanted, right?
To have all the time in the world
for my own work?

He goes out the door to where
we both worked for 30 years,
my soul is knocking around
there, but my body's here
brain had worn out at the tasks.
I have to *take back my soul.*

Come back, I'm here now
you should be too

This is like any life passage,
right? Birth, death, going to war,
marriage.

Well, let me tell you how those are different.

Birth: Suddenly, out you come!
In a body different than you'd understood
you thought you were fish,
or maybe reptile,
sensuously swimming, enjoying your
growing vertebrae   In there, lulled by
water, you had a soul—

263

Here, it's struggling to catch up,
trying to make the fit: this soul
with *this* body? Who said?
And who *are* all these creatures?
What if I don't like them? They're *loud.*
It's blurry, cold, clankety, much too bright.
Where's the water? You're not fish, but assume
you're good with air.
You aren't; gasp for breath.

Death.
No one gets *used* to death.
A one-way ticket. The more you prepare,
the better it can be.
I had too much radiation as a child
they were flagrant about dosage in the 50s,
now I hear about *brain scans for stroke victims.*
Badly trained technicians give 10 times
too much "to get a clearer image."

What? Did no one tell them that radiation
creates cancer? Radiation and brain tumors?
The FDA clueless again. They should work
with manufacturers to *not allow* the machine
to give a dose over a prescribed amount.

If someone ever has the bright idea of
a brain scan after a stroke for me, No *way.*
My death has already been hastened
by too much radiation.

Marriage: sadly, often
a holding camp for refugees.
Mutual rescue. Orphans embracing

one another; a bizarre arrangement.
Sometimes it works; not always.
People who can't stand on their own two feet
often marry the same. Sometimes one wakes up,
hits the road.

Ah—war. Kill or be killed: a strange job.
The likelihood of dying is more apparent
once you're over there, when it's too late.
You've become a killer hyped to kill
who may not be able to live with your children
in peacetime; you may battle addiction once
drugs are prescribed, not enough talk therapy

So here I am—home where I wanted to be.
Making friends with coyote and horses,
turning the compost, building the garden.
Dodging hunting accidents.

Stepping Back

I always knew it was coming—
it was obvious, a last day on the calendar,
a party on the next to last day,
still it seemed sudden, kind of
relentless—the way time moves on
no matter whether you're
Ready or Not!   *Here I come,* it says

There were tasks I meant to do
it became obvious that
if I didn't do them, someone else would.
Delegation was the order of the day.
No one cared. The world thrives on forward
movement.

Death will be like this—
no choice. A body wearing out.
Something you see coming.
Hopefully you can let go and let it happen
The finality suffusing you
a large wretched beast
mightier than you by far, impossible to fight.

How would you like to die?
Disease? Old age, sudden accident?
Stroke, heart attack. All possible.

The difference is I won't be on the other side,
writing about it.   Where will I be? Fairy's brow?
Gazing out the sleepy eyes of a kitten,
seeing I will grow into a cat?

A bull in the field near Bartleby's rock on Kauai,
switching my tail at flies?
Maybe just an ocean molecule
tirelessly lapping land in strong waves,
pulling sand from shore,
falling back.

What I Do in Maine

Today I went to the Library book sale
bought an armload of interesting books
then the thrift store
while R talked to the A Cappella guy next door
We drove up Seal Cove Road &
tried to psychically get the house he
wants reduced from 300K to 200K
picked blueberries got a method going to not spill any
on top of the world in a hidden place

Came home   ate   slept   wrote   ate dinner
planted tickweed, rose campion, bluebells
watered what I planted
Sat outside watching the sinuous fog come in
Imagined pulling up brush
in the lower overgrown flowerbed, bringing
compost & dirt to raise the level
pulled up some to see if this
would be easily done or madness
("Another bed? Haven't you got *enough*?")
He doesn't feel the allure of an old perennial bed

Noted that not only the picnic table needs new stain
& bulkhead doors need work
but white trim on every window's chipped to the wood.
There's the big expense of the summer.
I watched my perennial bed float away
among other needs   counters   painting the breezeway floor.

Summer Night

Human life is so different from other animals.
Their entire attention
          consumed by the need to procure food, fight for mates,
          consummate, birth their young, procure food for them.
Every single year.
Conditions are harsh for many.

The ways of all these are perilous.

Male antelope and wildebeest—
          every species of deer with a large rack
          crash their huge antlers,
          twist their necks, often get tangled together
          the victor has the pick of females.
Then one or the other or both must care for the young.
That's it.

None of this dreaming away   making art,
devising a spiritual life   creating relationships,
therapy   trying to sleep   finding joy

All summer we watch the five
disks of David Attenborough's "Planet Earth"
His sonorous tone: *If he doesn't catch this one, he will die*

The King father penguins shuffle along
holding one large egg warmly covered in fur
          between their legs,
          then huddle in a large circle,
          retaining warmth, inching sideways around

Their females are hundreds of miles away, eating,
free of babies for a while. The family's reunited,
then it starts all over again.

Natalia

These last days of July
I've felt a kind of backbone
spinal system to each day
more than ever before

my birth month
drawing to a close,
running to hold it back
from moving on to August
I like it—
I like my time
I like life
I want more

Deer Season

Middle of the night

Gunshot sounds in the far distance.
What is that?
There's no hunting in Acadia.
But not every acre is in the Park.
Random gunshots?

> Can you feel Divine Intelligence
> working through you?
> Be a vessel
> > for any star's light
> > to Earth

The Wake of the Wave

Can you look yourself in the mirror
can you fill your mouth with feathers
eating the untoward baby bird fallen too soon
out of its time; losing the domestic back to the wild

& so repairing a chink of the circle we have broken
& have no hope of ever rounding perfectly again;
can you put your finger up the asshole of Death
& not fear all your worlds tumbling down like
sapphire blocks, risking certain destruction
& still carry on with the experiments in glass

If there is mightiness here is it in the daytime?
Or does it only exist for you when you are asleep
can you let the dream speak directly
without having to put it through your
precious artistic voice

Can you love me with all the ambiguities
we offer the seashell? Hear the ocean roaring there
instead of trying to make it conform to some notion
of pattern learned from the past?

We've forsaken our families to make new ones
here in this starry turf, where we can see the sky,
feel water lapping our hands with inquiry

Endow all this as we will, it will all be over too soon
It is minimal anyway, in the vast spaces of
galaxies streaking into the timeless firmament

Seeing: To the Mailmen

I would wish, growing up
in a round dance
that if I made a picture
you would not dilute, ex-
tend, wash further
the colors beyond the border.

You would stop the eye there
and the sense given to the eye
by the eye; the colors therein
would remain therein
and not extend.

Even so, it would not be enough.
The picture would have to sing, not only
be seen; as an ocean or a far off
coyote is heard, the eye seeing
and the ear listening, breath & pulse
of the joy of living pushing out
through the chest and throat
to the world. Keep coyote
particularly in mind: full white chest,
head thrown back to the moon, his howl
a statement to all and the heavens—
outlasting Geronimo, the lion, the red wolf—
I am here. Know that I still exist.

A decent wish. Hoping for
a decent pleasure,
for the seer, whether watching
or hearing or reading,
loving or unloving.

Overwhelmed

> *—Daddy, what's a train? Is it something I can
> ride? Does it carry lots of girls 'n boys 'n
> grown-ups inside?*
> *—How can I explain?*
>
> —Utah Phillips

Life is not perfect.
You could cry at any moment.
Friday night, the weekend stretches long—
fabulous time, before Monday and work again.

Gang members kill
one another and innocent bystanders
in Oakland; lonely Goth teenagers
rage in Lakewood, Colorado

Young men's easy access to guns
stares us in the face; crippling this country

Fathers collect guns, hunt,
like their guns
they keep them under lock and key
train their young sons
how to load and fire a pistol in
a confusion of manhood
so the kid goes out and buys a gun
furious at his whole school scene
sprays the entire school with gunfire

Or there's no father at all around, the
gang's the family, in Mexico, Brazil, Oakland.

No gun cabinet under lock and key, just
a store which sells to anyone.
Oakland is dying. No jobs, no training, only
selling drugs. Schools don't reach these kids.

In the suburbs Mom goes to target practice
so she'll be safe; she feels like a guy
sturdy cool self-sufficient her cunning
small gun in her purse

You could cry at any moment

Because the gun lobby is unopposed
Because Charlton Heston played Moses,
standing on a mountain with a flowing beard,
arms uplifted, holding the Ten Commandments
People see him as *The God of Guns*
like his tough western persona which
gives authority to the concept of a citizen's
"right to bear arms," an idea left over from 1776.
They contribute to the NRA
thinking only of defending themselves.

They aren't seeing the escalation of violence in
the whole society, don't relate to the problem
as a whole

We're the only industrialized nation
in the world with such a lack of
gun control. Most European countries
don't allow guns in their borders.

How can a gun lobby be stronger than
a government?

Because the government is involved
in selling guns itself; the military dominates.

A culture of war—fighting easier than diplomacy.

These are the same characters
who sold arms to third world nations for the
last hundred years, who armed Iraq and Pakistan,
guns spilling into every country:
Liberia? Check.
South Africa? Check.
Somalia? Check.

African despots set up against their own people
with the arms they've bought from us
Pakistan fighting us with arms we sold them

This is Obama's heritage
beginning with Eisenhower
who funded *the best and the brightest*
in my childhood to develop nuclear weapons,
didn't foresee nuclear winter
in a pell-mell intoxication with
capitalism and détente.
Throw back the cocktails! Want a martini?
How 'bout a Valium?

You could cry at any moment
and do
Because these problems are out of control
because so many of the world's poor
hardly have a chance.

We need clean oceans, streams, ponds, air
Enough food   shelter   livelihood
for everyone.

Each problem is complex, has to be teased out
one at a time and solved

Despots and ruling elites hog land
and the means of production.
Then a natural disaster like an earthquake in
Haiti or hurricanes and floods in Pakistan
threatens countries which couldn't
feed their people before

Life is not perfect.
You could cry at any moment,
and do,
because no matter how much we love you
It isn't enough.

Ways to Sleep

Others too are
stuck in dark rooms &
dark houses; wakeful, watching,
praying for sleep.

Get up & use the golden time.

If you're young and the neighborhood is safe,
go for a run at 3:30 a.m.
I ply the house, go downstairs,
sit around reading. Play with the cat.

Some nights it works—no herbs, no drugs,
& that is magic. Fills me with hope.

Assume that people love you. You are not alone.
Even if it's death by accident
the waters of your death will be warm
You'll glide into the next bardo
in satiny sleep, loving your dreams,
seeing others, pillows bearing you
towards everlasting time.

Chant, prostrations, yoga, sit.

Empty stomach.
Console yourself: Maybe Sarah Orne Jewett
and Edith Wharton became lovers
in this very house. Maybe it was a safe
house, a friend no one knew, the
cousin of a sister.

Make friends with bats, cats, crayfish, spiders,
who slip, sidle, slide, and fly. They surround.
You are never alone.

Three a Triangle

1

A ship needs
Chance swimming alongside its
hull, brushing by its
bulk, dipping & bobbing by its
moorings when in port—
Needs this as much as mast & consciousness

Sails with slight uncertainty in the
bones of the sailors, into adventure
calms & squalls   sometimes it seems just too far
Over shoals among rocks outside blue hot city nights
green slow days of undercurrent movement

Don't you think, Richard, we are ship
& also waves   coming into a cove   sand on the shore,
the finer particles of salt & grainy sand diffusing our nature
receiving & traveling & staying to be penetrated
in our lives & bodies & the guts of the poem

This gravitational pull between one another
is the way we be
like moon pulling tide
dashing light and wave onto each other
sometimes only a fine spray
An otherwise gentle sluice
sinking into sand.

Take the rhythm
of the days, streaming down into one another
sliding across the shore before the eye

I want to determine the measure yet
must be variable as fucking hours are
when we feed like big sperm whales
We three—mother, father, baby
spraying sandy love over our torsos

We'd better keep
a record of our great voyages, rounding the tip of
Cape Horn off Tierra del Fuego, this violent strip of
chaotic waters

You hadn't known you could continue
to see bees dancing the wall
long after their shadows were gone.

Nor had the play the sun makes
on Robin's calm face
been revealed before it was noted. Who reads the
record? We counted on nothing. The sand
doesn't count on the tides for penetration;
I am too experienced at the game now to count on you.
Your mind did not assume it would record the bees
in any of the ways (shadows, dance, drones, Queen)
it did. Let the blessed child on the Sun Card
riding the white horse,
be triumphant.
Dark waters, dark Chance: our tiny boat
plying the deep vast ocean.

2

Love will speak its brilliance as often as
its deformities; intellectual laziness
will cascade out of misshapen temples
dedicated to weak images of woman-goddess.
  Love will out,
when it is ready, but you have to nurture it
a shy fellow   goes back in, if not gentled along

We work; are replenished in
the very doing

3

A flattery to think we
have anything to do
with the forces
of expulsion

The contraction (the orgasm
takes hold, forces with tidal energy
pressure against the cervix
The disease
takes hold; other bacteria
marshal against it if we leave
it alone in a sterile environment

She must be in the middle of a
labor pain. The orgasm emerges from the
forest of the poem tearing through order
She likes expulsion, things that burst out
or burst in, likes the lack of control
and excitement from friction

The poem
(returning to it, as record of a moving field)
is like rubbing sticks together to make fire
creating a mood one
has been seeking

The words bring on
whole chunks of the day, quickly eat time
You have something—you're further ahead
than you were before

On my arm a colony of streptococci
waves in the early evening breeze
On the tip of my tongue
always words; more recently—silence.

4

Secure corners:
                    I studied in a corner in the
basement at college with an L made by two
desks perpendicular. Chair, books, notebooks
both desks arranged around me. The walls enclosed
our desks bordered my thoughts rationed
my feelings

Margaret sat cross-legged on her bed
in her room, halo of red hair above her
thin white nightgown
drinking cokes empty bottles lined up
Studying for history & bio tests: every three
hours took a break, making lists of
dates. I was lousy at this. Neither of us

had a large chance of remembering
and had no idea of our own history

                    5

The sea dashes against the shore
soaking the sand each time,
lapping.

Women lap at the shore,
a force, like waves.
Not a shoot, not direct;
gradual. A thousand tiny acts
over a day.

Nursing the baby, heavy fabulous feeling
of milk letting down.   Feeling his sperm
Being held by him   Cuddling the baby
Cuddling with him   Impatient with him
Arguing with him   Watching him and the baby
sleep   Growing into Robin   Feeling R is down
he knows I know it   will no longer pretend

Robin's hands a fist they are a bit clammy
have spots on them   R's hands
& sperm all over my belly
Urine seeping into my shorts & shirt
Sleepy when the lights go on, R wraps
the blanket around himself   turns away from me

Blinking at the light punched on, Robin
delivers a grunt then a burp—I have
waited for that. He meets the morning

& the slightly infirm cat who sits by him
with a loopy smile, drawing on my breast,
he sucks his hand for a moment
when it grazes his face, the thumb is tightly inside,
undifferentiated as yet

My tongue is agile
& knows its way; my cheeks get tired.
We are both masters at sucking.
Daylight opens the blue curtains.
The orange titan spills lemon raindrops
over the Polar Cap.

Forest Song: Cat off Green Island

Spindle is a foggy grey
short-haired cat, strong male explorer
haunts the shore, moves through the forests
       If not Spindle's island,
no one's

He watches the flickering coal eyes
of a black bird

Peers out at the slop, slop
       slow swish
of long canoes with many paddles
moving up the Sound
to Somes Pond

The Penobscot are clamming & hunting
these summers beneath suede-covered mountains
watching us as we watch them

Later, Spindle picks his way through the forest,
flushing woodcocks   tansy nodding, dislodged
   by his grey pads

taking aim on each mouse   he's riveted:
then pounces   hot blood   toss, play
of the kill

Columbus Day is my father's birthday.
This year, 1969, he's been divorced a year
Here his day is the heart of hunting season
Each man takes his part of the

"harvest"—a ghastly word legitimizing this "sport"
We have to watch our step in the October kill
no hunting in Acadia but hard to know
where the park stops   life's in danger outside

Just don't you kill my cat Spindle
or my father

The Nature of Love

Not to remain totally free
        but uncluttered
as though time itself were moving
        down a continuum of consciousness
marking its pace by piecing conundrums
        together in this house:
walking through two bedrooms, a kitchen,
        meeting the different smells
of each, different shade of temperature

Orange fall quiet of afternoon wind
        blowing through trees, filtering time
In this isolation, no house but ours
        in the woods, no lives to live but ours in
the ingredients of each day

Red rug in the baby's bedroom,
        kitchen hot with bubbling stew,
cats in the living room windows
        He cries
from a blister on his arm
        from trying to raise himself
at three months
        in this heavy world.

Wild Horses, Wild Dreams

—Schooner Gulch, above Anchor Bay, Mendocino Coast

Jacqueline moved onto land
where a herd of wild horses already lived

It became obvious they were no one's,
had drifted up and down this coast
for years, a bother to many.
They were not a bother to her.
Something—A past life? Destiny?
placed her here with them *for* them,
a match made in the glory of the foggy coast

A pinto herd: six, a new foal, and a filly
born last spring. They come
when J calls, *to the food,* she says; *maybe a bit,*
my voice now. They're wary; she wants
to get them used to new people.

Pintos have one blue eye, one brown.
The big black dominant male has
ostracized another male from
the herd. We go next door
and feed Little One; there's an empty
fenced ring there.

She walks and calls for him, then suddenly
he's on our left, appears out of nowhere.
If he keeps being driven out of the herd,
I might break and ride him—but far off.

These horses have a magical air about them—
from their freedom, I think, their
knowledge that they have her eighty-eight acres
and her neighbor's three hundred next door.
They chew moistened alfalfa cubes
from a flat hand with their huge teeth,
thick half-broken carrots. New foal with no teeth
snuffles against my palm.

The rest kick each other, circle around.
I stand back, trying to be in clear view
of any who care, not in kicking range.
I'm no harm, I want them to know.
Their size is substantial. They're out here
in rain, strong wind from the immediate
ocean, the dense fog. *They wouldn't like it inside,*
J says.   Under nearby trees for cover, they're prey
for two bobcats and a brown bear.
They stick around near water's edge.
J's gotten good fences so they don't straggle
down onto the highway, get themselves killed,
her sued.

Their big eyes are serious. They look at you with no
guile. That's why she loves them
there's no intrigue of human interaction.
An eye on each side of the head.
Lose an eye, that whole side's blind.

To be wild means to not trust anything, anyone,
fend for one's self. The oldest is seventeen.
Now they've got Jacqueline looking after them,
first time ever they've had *anyone* other than
Can you get these damn horses off my land!

Patches of white against brown.
Pintos were the favored horse of Ute and Navahos
introduced by early European settlers from Spain

They back too close to one another and kick,
stir up trouble. J points to the rump
of one's been nipped a lot, beveled scarred flanks.
Two males in a herd = trouble.

I know what *I* dream
I'm hungry for—
the dreams of wild horses.

Wildebeest and Crocodile

The wildebeest come to drink at the river,
they've traveled hundreds of miles
to the Sahara Delta fanning out in spring,
    but waiting for them—
are crocodiles!

Is it that they forget? Or know, and
just so thirsty they *have* to drink?
It's inevitable:
the large antelope dips his head to the cool water,
a good long draught, the crocodile rises up
sinks a huge set of teeth into a leg.

The wildebeest can't make it back up the cliff—
the death is brutal and horrible.
He is pulled, toppled, into the river
the croc swims off, dragging its prey.

That's the theme of "Planet Earth,"
David Attenborough's massive film.
As animals trek hundreds of miles
to find their food, either conditions are
deteriorating from climate change
or other beasts are tracking *them*

For most predators there is another
higher in the Chain of Being/
evolutionary ladder, except for crocodiles—
nothing threatens them
except humans, and polluted rivers.

Humans threaten every species. Wildebeest
(also known as gnu) are trapped by poachers
and sold. Eastern plains gnu are now almost extinct,
in South Africa they're protected by law.

The snow leopard, living high up in precipices
of the Himalayas, is so rare he becomes even
more valuable to native poachers—

Feed your people, is Attenborough's pitch,
so they won't endanger other species.
One wonders—if the monetary motive to hunt is removed,
will people still hunt for tribal affiliation,
because this is what defines a man?
Can these governments really create other jobs?

A Radiant Being

He came to Berkeley imported
by me for an author program,
swam in our house for two days
treading our waters, our rhythms

there was talk—
He did Reiki work on clients
far from here
without picking up the phone
I'd see him staring into space,
either doing it or
thinking his thoughts

We both grew up in Colorado,
I from Denver, he from Craig on the
western slope, a ranching family—
cattle and wheat, he said

Where would you most like to live
if not Mesa, Arizona? I asked

Rumania, he answered, describing
how he flowed with his friends
like jeweled waves through the evening
a level of acceptance
and camaraderie there

The last morning I got up and waited
for the early shuttle with him—
puttered around the kitchen
like a mom seeing off a son on a trip.

He stood alone, beatific in the living room—
for a moment our John from Cincinnati—
then said he'd wait outside.
I hoped the Bayporter wouldn't be late.

Coming up the hill like a steed, lights flashed long—
It slowed, driver peering at numbers.
He waved to the driver and
was scooped up; fetched.
I climbed the stars to sleep.

Insouciant Elephant

Wild mind leaping
tricking itself and you,
among dizzying mirrors
distancing you from everything,
tearing yourself down by a zillion
fears—
Stop it. Reach to
something life-giving,
holy

My body has to be
lulled to sleep, not so much
seduced as beckoned

>A game my family used to play:
>adults and children hid in the absolute dark
>among hulking pieces of furniture
>everything common slightly scary
>"I Want A Beckon" meant *give me a hint*
>We ranged over the whole house, upstairs
>and down. I loved this game,
>loved my parents for so gamely playing it,
>the way it had nothing
>to do with anything utilitarian

And now:
I need to beckon my insouciant elephant
A quiet, mysterious summons of the soul
to dream   Sometimes it happens but often
I can't find it   a *locus* missing in my own body

I put down A. L. Kennedy's *Paradise,* a novel
I fiercely love about alcoholism
sample Tsoknyi Rinpoche's
Fearless Simplicity and *Carefree Dignity*
Which shall it be? To train and calm
the awakened mind—"the atmosphere within which
all difficulties naturally dissolve."

The solution is a bath, but it's loud.
Something great about the pounding water.
Neither see nor say. See everything, say
nothing—ride the crest of the wave,
slide down. A month to go, the last month.
Then she will be free, she will dance
and prance. Revel in her name
backwards: YDNIL.

As a child my family
played games over the years,
some using our names backwards.
Known and called for days by these
otherworldly monikers.

This happened at Central City, near Georgetown
a summer house amid gold mine shafts from 1856
mine buildings, tailings piles—
hillsides otherwise
covered with soft evergreens, deep crevices and
canyons, bubbling streams we played in.

See and say
YMMOM, KNAH, EISUS, YLLOP.
Our names, for weeks.
Almost forgotten. Then I would take the

trash down the mountainside to dump in the
mine shaft, and someone would yell, YDNIL!
It made you laugh, your dad calling your name
backwards.
Sixty years later you thought of it,
wandering in the caves of memory,
and laughed again, lolling in the bath.

Later she wondered if
she'd superimposed memory on memory:
Were these names played with in her *own*
family, NIBOR and ADNARIM,
HCIR, YDNIL again? Did her natal family even do it?
Did they both do it? A running stream, a brook
of lively birdsong through the generations.
A waltz   better than fine.

Thursday Night at Saul's

If you cry too much here
your dad will whisk you outside.
Even if you howl all the way
I don't wanna go!

Be instead the twenty-year-olds,
secure and jaunty in their
social worlds, snug as
a nightie, held by arms
which also don't always do
what they want

or be that eighty-year-old
doggedly eating his latkes & brisket,
trying to maintain a shred of dignity
his heart chipping into fragments that
his wife hasn't looked up from her Bible
or spoken in fifteen minutes

All the next meals will be the same.
In five years he won't come here anymore
too many cans of soup in the fridge,
keys in the dog's dish, everything misplaced,
including people. The x-rays show
a cottage cheese brain.

She went fast, though the four years
seemed like forever.
Now his friends try to get him here
with them: "C'mon, how about Saul's?
You used to like that place."

"Nope, sad associations," he says brusquely,
telling them on the way to Solano
that after that night
he vowed never to go back.

It's my fantasy that the waiter and manager
are lovers. They walk around
appraising the state of things,

but no, I see now he's a new busboy
being trained by a waiter—"Clear table 7 next."
We're a grid. Their moves among our tables
deft and choreographed as a figure skater's
long set— "8, 4 and 6." His world is cleaning
and pouring water, bringing the initial pickle.

This is his start, a freshman at Cal.
He will he stay on, outlast other staff,
buy out the owners. Ten years
& two other restaurants sees him
selling Saul's, moving to Dubai.
His wife leaves him and marries the son of a Yemini
imam friendly with Al Qaeda. This Berkeley High
girl, a punk lesbian
when he first dated her
begins to wear the hijab, drops out of touch

He and his new wife move to London in their
last years. He thinks of Saul's, his wild
crush on the energetic manager who first
told him *a restaurant is a grid: 8, 4 and 6.*
The amazing nights they churned in bed
amid calls from the manager's initially frantic,
then deploring & sarcastic wife as

August fog blew wisps up to the hills
like something out of "Vertigo."
How the manager dropped him flat/broke his heart
when he said the square of the grid
he wanted to live in
was Palestine.

Photo by Jon Haeber

Lindy Hough is the author of four books of poetry and edited *Nuclear Strategy and the Code of the Warrior*. She and her husband Richard Grossinger founded the literary magazine *Io* in the mid-1960s and North Atlantic Books in the early 1970s, where she was for many years Publisher and Editorial Director. She lives in Berkeley, California.

The Io Poetry Series

The Io Poetry Series honors the career work of poets who express the depth, breadth, and scope of subject matter of *Io* and North Atlantic Books. The Series pays tribute to North Atlantic Books' literary roots in *Io*, the inter-disciplinary journal founded by Lindy Hough, Richard Grossinger, and colleagues in 1964. *Io*'s single-subject issues laid the groundwork for North Atlantic Books' literary publishing of subsequent decades. The poets in this series either appeared in the journal, were working concurrently, or preceded and inspired *Io*.

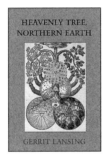

Heavenly Tree, Northern Earth
GERRIT LANSING

The Intent On
KENNETH IRBY

Westport Poems
JONATHAN TOWERS

Wild Horses, Wild Dreams:
New and Selected Poems 1971–2010
LINDY HOUGH